S0-BTL-320

Your Movie Guide To

SCIENCE FICTION/ FANTASY

VIDEO TAPES AND DISCS

By the Editors of
VIDEO TIMES MAGAZINE

Written by Tim Lucas and the contributing editors of *Video Times* magazine.

The photographs in this book are courtesy of the following studios and organizations:
Universal-International Pictures Corp.; Cineman Syndicate; Walt Disney Productions; Media Home Entertainment; Movie Star News; Museum of Modern Art/Film Stills Archive; 20th Century-Fox Film Corp.; Avco Embassy Pictures; MGM/UA; Columbia Pictures Industries, Inc.; United Artists; Associated Film Distribution; Vestron Video; MCA Home Video; Thorn EMI Video Programming Enterprises; Paramount Pictures Corp.; Warner Brothers, Inc.

Printed in Canada

INTRODUCTION

Movies can do wonderful things. They can entertain us, lift us out of sadness, and help us forget our worries. But one of their greatest abilities is to take us to places and into situations which do not and may never exist. To make the impossible seem possible is the specific purpose behind science fiction and fantasy films.

The amazing popularity of science fiction and fantasy films today insures them wide representation on videotapes and discs. The titles collected in this book extend from the earliest dabblings in special effects by science fiction pioneer Georges Méliès to *Dune,* with the middle era represented by such milestones as *Metropolis* (1925), *Things to Come* (1936), *Forbidden Planet* (1956), *The Time Machine* (1960), and the genre's supreme accomplishment, *2001: A Space Odyssey* (1968). Current titles are being released all the time, supplemented by the occasional classic—of which *Them!* (1954) is a perfect, recent example. Oddly enough, the one science fiction film that predicted videotape as a part of man's future—Byron Haskin's *Robinson Crusoe on Mars* (1964)—remains unavailable!

As with the other volumes in this series, we must delete certain titles which may possess science fiction or fantasy content but seem more representative of a different genre. Good examples are Disney's *Alice in Wonderland* and *Darby O'Gill and the Little People* (which can be found in the *Children's* volume), and nearly all of the Monty Python features (which are in the *Comedy* book). On the other hand, if science fiction has been judged inseparable from a film's character, as in Woody Allen's comedy *Sleeper* or Disney's *The Absent-Minded Professor,* the film was included here.

In 1895, H. G. Wells wrote about a machine that could launch a human being backwards and forwards in time. In 1985, videocassette and laserdisc players are as close as we have come to realizing his vision. They grant us the ability to revisit the gems (and the rusty clunkers) of the past, and science fiction and fantasy tapes and discs are the accessories which allow us the alternative of forward movement.

ABSENT-MINDED PROFESSOR, THE (1961) B/W. *Dir.:* Robert Stevenson. *With:* Fred MacMurray, Nancy Olson, Keenan Wynn. **97 mins.** Beta, VHS **($69.95)**; Laser **($34.95)**; CED **($19.95)**. Disney. ★★★½

A college science prof invents "flubber," a miracle, antigravity substance that helps his car to fly and puts a spring into the step of the local basketball team. Probably the Disney Studios' finest live-action feature, it showcases an array of memorable characters and absolutely *uplifting* special effects shots (one puts you inside the shoes of a man bouncing higher than his house!). A must for man, woman, and child.

ADVENTURES OF BUCKAROO BANZAI, THE (1983) C. *Dir.:* W.D. Richter. *With:* Peter Weller, John Lithgow, Jeff Goldblum. **103 mins.** Rated PG. Beta Hi-Fi, VHS Hi-Fi **($79.95)**; Laser; CED. Vestron. ★★½

Weird, downright deliberate cult movie rotates around universal talents of heroic Banzai (Weller), a neurosurgeon/physics theorist/rock guitarist/black belt/daredevil. While testing an invention that allows him to burrow through solid matter, B.B. discovers an 8th Dimension race of monsters that inconspicuously invaded Earth during Orson Welles' phony *War of the Worlds* broadcast. Lithgow is positively mondo as demented Dr. Lizardo, but the film is too overburdened with offbeat sights and sounds to be easily digested.

ADVENTURES OF CAPTAIN MARVEL, THE (1941) B/W. *Dir.:* William Witney and John English. *With:* Tom Tyler, Frank Coghlan, Jr., William Benedict. **240 mins.** No rating. Beta, VHS **($N/A).** Nostalgia Merchant. ★★★

This renowned, 12-episode serial is simply the best of its kind—suspenseful, funny, and endearingly naive. Billy Batson is given the secret code word "Shazam!" by the Gods which, when uttered, endows him with all their greatest virtues (i.e., the wisdom of Solomon, the strength of Zeus, etc.). Tyler, one of Universal's cowboy stars, played the Mummy without screen credit in *The Mummy's Hand* the same year.

ADVENTURES OF ULTRAMAN, THE (1981) C. *Dir.:* Eiji Tsuburaya. *Animated*. **90 mins.** No rating. Beta, VHS **($59.95).** Family Home Entertainment. ★★

By flashing his "Beta capsule," a mortal is transformed into the giant superhero of title, an ideal solution to Tokyo's constant problem of town-stomping monsters. Made up of episodes from a popular Japanese teleseries, this mindless fun was masterminded by special-effects wizard Tsuburaya *(Godzilla, Rodan, Mysterians)*. It's sold as a children's tape, but effects mavens will find this passable entertainment.

AGENCY (1981) C. *Dir.:* George Kaczender. *With:* Robert Mitchum, Lee Majors, Valerie Perrine. **94 mins.** Rated R. Beta, VHS **($79.95);** CED **($29.98).** Vestron. ★★
Advertising executive Majors accidentally penetrates a high-echelon level of secrecy at his agency and discovers his company's president (Mitchum) is lacing his work with dangerous subliminal imagery. Bears slight similarity to another Canadian film *Videodrome,* but has none of the other's wit and imagination. Features good support from Saul Rubinek.

ALIEN (1979) C. *Dir.:* Ridley Scott. *With:* Sigourney Weaver, Tom Skerritt, John Hurt, Harry Dean Stanton. **116 mins.** Rated R. Beta, VHS **($59.95);** Laser **($34.98);** CED **($19.98).** CBS/Fox. ★★★
Scary space adventure shamelessly culled from several SF cult movies (i.e., *Planet of the Vampires, It! The Terror From Beyond Space)* has space-barge crew contending with stowaway monstrosity. Top-notch acting, imaginative production design, and director Scott's eye for detail flatter a bland script, resulting in one of the most genuinely harrowing films of its type.

ALIEN CONTAMINATION (1981) C. *Dir.:* Lewis Coates (Luigi Cozzi). *With:* Ian McCulloch, Louise Monroe. **90 mins.** Rated R. Beta, VHS **($64.95).** Paragon Video Productions. ★★
An interplanetary space vehicle returns to earth with a cargo of strange eggs which proceed to hatch. This Italian *Alien* rip-off is less of a groaner than director Coates' other work (see *Hercules*), helped by the silly frenzy of the situation and a pulsating rock score by The Goblins.

ALIEN FACTOR, THE (1978) C. *Dir.:* Donald M. Dohler. *With:* Don Leifert, Tom Griffiths, George Stover. **82 mins.** Rated PG. Beta, VHS **($59.95).** VCI. ★

Monstrous predators from space victimize Earth. It's as banal as that, and filmed no more expertly than the average home movie. Appropriately, the director is the editor of *Cinemagic,* a magazine catering to amateur filmmakers. A poor investment, even as a rental.

ALIENS FROM SPACESHIP EARTH (1977) C. *With:* Donovan, Lynda Day George. **107 mins.** Rated PG. Beta, VHS **($59.95).** Video Gems. ★

One of those semi-documentaries about visitations from extraterrestrials, full of narrated case histories and dramatic reenactments of various close encounters. Only those who are absolutely starving for the slightest sliver of science fiction should bother. What was sixties rocker Donovan thinking, making his acting debut in this tabloid turkey?

ALPHA INCIDENT, THE (1977) C. *Dir.:* Bill Debane. *With:* Ralph Meeker and Stafford Morgan. **86 mins.** Rated PG. Beta, VHS **($59.95).** Media. ★

A shipment of "dangerous cells" is accidentally spilled en route to Denver, contaminating four railroad workers with an unexplained disease that will cause their brains to explode at the onset of sleep. Film never condescends to explain the wheres and whys of the situation, so the viewer is given nothing solid on which to base his interest. This is one movie that won't keep you awake.

ALPHAVILLE (1965) B/W. *Dir.:* Jean-Luc Godard. *With:* Eddie Constantine, Anna Karina, Howard Vernon. **100 mins.** No rating. Beta, VHS. **($55.00).** Festival. ★★★

Lemmy Caution, the hard-boiled detective hero of several low-grade French thrillers, was elevated to art in this genuinely weird, depressing vision. Godard cleverly adapts the character to his own experimental ends, assigning him to another galaxy where he must rescue a scientific genius ruled by his own race of robots. The future depicted here is computer controlled, peopled with faceless men and iconographic women, and looks a lot like 1965.

ALTERED STATES (1980) C. *Dir.:* Ken Russell. *With:* William Hurt, Blair Brown, Charles Haid. **103 mins.** Rated R. Beta, VHS **($59.95);** Laser **($29.98);** CED **($19.98).** Warner. ★★★

Scientist Hurt, exploring venues of altered consciousness, dabbles in tribal drug rituals and sensory deprivation tanks until his mental changes begin to affect him in physical ways. Absolutely brilliant except for the ridiculous midsection, when Hurt is briefly transformed into a deer-eating Neanderthal man, and the disappointingly sudden (and unbelievable) resolution. Russell's trademark visual excess seems born for this sort of material and scores several bulls-eyes, but also led author Paddy Chayefsky to remove his name from the film.

ANDROID (1983) C. *Dir.:* Aaron Lipstadt. *With:* Klaus Kinski, Brie Howard, Don Opper. **80 mins.** Rated PG. Beta, VHS **($69.95).** Media. ★★½

Three escaped space convicts dock with a craft where a doctor of biomechanics (Kinski) is preparing a female android to replace his present assistant, a cyborg named Max 404. Complications occur when both the creator and his sex-obsessed assistant notice that one of their aggressive visitors is female. Interesting, low-key film was overrated by some mainstream critics, thanks to the personable but dorky android hero. Dedicated followers of the genre won't notice many significant steps being made here.

ANDROMEDA STRAIN, THE (1971) C. *Dir.:* Robert Wise. *With:* Arthur Hill, David Wayne, James Olson. **131 mins.** Rated G. Beta, VHS **($59.95)** MCA. ★★★

Based on a Michael Crichton story about a fatal virus spreading insidiously from a fallen satellite and draining all life from the immediate area—with a couple of intriguing exceptions. Tension mounts as research scientists test the immunity of two survivors to a lethal space micro-organism in a blindingly sterile, subterranean complex. A sterling combination of SF and against-the-clock suspense; the film's cold veneer makes nullity of space look warm by comparison.

ANGEL OF H.E.A.T. (1982) C. *Dir.:* Myril A. Schreibman. *With:* Marilyn Chambers, Mary Woronov. **90 mins.** Rated R. Beta, VHS **($69.95);** Laser **($29.95);** CED **($29.95).** Vestron. ★★

This soft-core espionage fantasy features Chambers as Angel Harmony (head of Harmony's Elite Attack Team), tackling a mad scientist and his army of robots. Diverting on many counts, it's basically an okay time. The supporting presence of Woronov *(Eating Raoul)* as Angel's lesbian cohort helps a lot.

ANGEL ON MY SHOULDER (1946) B/W. *Dir.:* Archie Mayo. *With:* Paul Muni, Claude Rains, Anne Baxter. **100 mins.** No rating. Beta, VHS **($19.95)**. Crown, Kartes, VCI. ★★½

Muni is a murdered mobster who makes a deal with Satan and is restored to life in the body of a judge who has won Satan's disfavor by putting too many criminals on the road to redemption. In his new guise, he sets about avenging his own death and scheming his way clear of an eternity in hell. This typical Hollywood angle on fantasy is lifted out of mundaneness by a good combination of actors and an inventively presented sequence in hell.

ANIMAL FARM (1955) C. *Dir.:* John Halas and Joy Batchelor. *Animated.* **73 mins.** No rating. Beta, VHS **($44.95)**. Video Yesteryear. ★★★

George Orwell's classic political allegory about an animal revolt against the pigs who pen them is cleverly transformed into a stylized animation piece. Made in England, it has a look reminiscent of, but suitably darker in mood than, Disney's features. There is a trace of unevenness, probably budgetary in nature, and a new ending which Orwell probably wouldn't have approved of.

ANNA TO THE INFINITE POWER (1984) C. *Dir.:* Robert Wiemer. *With:* Dina Merrill, Martha Byrne, Jack Gilford. **108 mins.** No rating. Beta Hi-Fi, VHS **($59.95)**. RCA/Columbia. ★

An obnoxious girl discovers she is one of five clones of a dead scientist, a fact she shouldn't have learned until puberty. Why is Anna not only bright, but a kleptomaniac? What is the secret of her sadistic piano teacher? These and other questions are inanely answered by an almost supernaturally inept movie.

AT THE EARTH'S CORE (1976) C. *Dir.:* Kevin Connor. *With:* Doug McClure, Peter Cushing, Caroline Munro. **90 mins.** Rated PG. Beta, VHS **($59.95)**. Warner. ★½

This chintzy Edgar Rice Burroughs adaptation from England's Amicus Productions follows Victorian scientists in a giant boring (it drills, too) device to a subterranean, monster-enslaved civilization. McClure is thick and uncharismatic, and Cushing's fidgety-old-man routine is, from such a fine actor, a shocking display. The film would be unendurable if not for its sultry heroine Munro and laughable special effects.

ATOR THE FIGHTING EAGLE (1983) C. *Dir.:* David Hills. *With:* Miles O'Keefe, Sabrina Siami, Warren Hillman. **98 mins.** Rated PG. Beta, VHS **($69.95).** Thorn EMI. ★

Ator, son of Thorn, wages a barbarian war against the "tragic dynasty of the Spider." This is overinflated sword-and-sorcery nonsense that borrows freely from everything but the bank that financed its frequent special effects.

ATTACK OF THE 50-FOOT WOMAN (1958) B/W. *Dir.:* Nathan Hertz (Juran). *With:* Allison Hayes, Yvette Vickers, William Hudson. **66 mins.** No rating. Beta, VHS **($39.98).** Key. ★

In an hour of pure camp, Hayes encounters a giant alien, is called a drunk in front of an entire town, and becomes a giantess in a bedsheet bikini on the warpath for her womanizing husband, Harry. The ultimate low-budget SF extravaganza!

AUDREY ROSE (1977) C. *Dir.:* Robert Wise. *With:* Anthony Hopkins, Marsha Mason, Susan Swift. **113 mins.** Rated PG. Beta, VHS **($59.95).** MGM/UA. ★★

A 12-year-old girl's trance-like nightmares are clarified when a stranger (Hopkins) shows up to claim her as the reincarnation of his own daughter. The potentially interesting plot is allowed to run amok, with the film culminating in a lawsuit that must prove or disprove the reality of reincarnation! One of director Wise's many recent backfires, based on one of Frank De Felitta's many forgettable reincarnation potboilers.

BAMBOO SAUCER, THE (1968) C. *Dir.:* Frank Telford. *With:* Dan Duryea, Lois Nettleton, John Ericson. **100 mins.** No rating. Beta, VHS **($39.95).** Republic. ★★★

A scientific expedition seeks out a flying saucer that has landed in Tibet, unaware that an impromptu trip to Saturn awaits them. An odd cast for an SF film, to be sure, but the equally odd setting and characters lift an otherwise ordinary story out of its inherent doldrums. Acceptable time killer.

BARBARELLA (1968) C. *Dir.:* Roger Vadim. *With:* Jane Fonda, John Phillip Law, David Hemmings. **98 mins.** Rated PG. Beta, VHS **($24.95);** Laser **($29.95);** CED **($19.98).** Paramount. ★★½

Fonda's major career oddity finds her cast as a 41st century sextronaut in pursuit of scientist Durand Durand. This movie is utterly unlike anything else Vadim has made, with a beguiling air of artificiality that makes it more closely resemble Fellini on one of his off days. An overly brash musical score and eye-straining, psychedelic visual effects ultimately cause the film to overstay its welcome.

BARON MUENCHAUSEN (1943) C. *Dir.:* Josef von Baky. *With:* Hans Albers, Hermann Speelmans, Kaethe Kaack. **110 mins.** Subtitled. No rating. Beta, VHS **($79.95).** Video City. ★★★★
One of the finest achievements of the German fantasy cinema, ironically produced by the Nazi Party under the watchful eye of General Joseph Goebbels. The film follows its charismatic hero on adventures extending from Turkish harems to the lunar surface. The script is jam-packed with such elegant trickery as invisibility, riding cannonballs through the air, and characters that remove their heads from their bodies.

BATTLE BENEATH THE EARTH (1968) C. *Dir.:* Montgomery Tully. *With:* Peter Arne, Robert Ayers, Kerwin Mathews. **112 mins.** No rating. Beta, VHS **($59.95).** MGM/UA. ★★
Fanatical renegades from mainland China burrow under the Pacific Ocean to the United States, planning to control the world with atomic blackmail. Amusingly corny dialogue and obviously forged Orientals (wouldn't authentic ones participate?) make this low-grade production endearing in spite of itself.

BATTLE BEYOND THE STARS (1980) C. *Dir.:* Jimmy T. Murakami. *With:* Richard Thomas, John Saxon, George Peppard. **103 mins.** Rated PG. Beta, VHS **($69.95);** CED **($29.95).** Vestron. ★★★
John Sayles scripted this space parody of *The Magnificent Seven* (with Robert Vaughn reprising his earlier role!), which follows Thomas' struggle to protect his pacific planet from invading ogre Saxon. As with any Roger Corman production, the special effects are cheap and serviceable, but it's the film's *human* element that makes the whole appealing. Corman reportedly snipped much of the original cut's comedy prior to release; fortunately, some things got past him.

BATTLESTAR GALACTICA (1978) C. *Dir.:* Richard A. Colla. *With:* Lorne Greene, Dirk Benedict, Richard Hatch. **125 mins.** Rated PG. Beta, VHS **($79.95);** Laser **($29.98);** CED **($19.98).** MCA. ★★½

This feature consists of two trimmed-down, slightly altered episodes of the short-lived ABC-TV series, documenting the space-age dogfights of the titular vehicle and the marauding Cylons. Of course, it wouldn't exactly be television without some tedious, tame romance with Jane Seymour! John Dykstra's neat special effects, as well as the tightened narrative, were better appreciated during this version's initial large-screen, (and Sensurround!) exhibitions, but video's limitations reduce this production to its original basics.

Battlestar Galactica

The Beastmaster

BEASTMASTER, THE (1982) C. *Dir.:* Don Coscarelli. *With:* Marc Singer, Tanya Roberts, Rip Torn. **119 mins.** Rated PG. Beta, VHS **($79.95);** Laser **($34.95);** CED **($29.98).** MGM/UA. ★★

Coscarelli's success with his first film, *Phantasm,* led to this mid-budget, sword-and-sorcery tale, an overmild, comparative letdown. Singer is the infant survivor of tribal genocide who, birthed by a cow, grows to well-muscled maturity with the ability to communicate with all animals. This skill comes in handy in combat against Maax (Torn), diabolical cultist and slaughterer of his people. Using Torn and Kubrick cinematographer John Alcott on material like this is like adding good wine to canned soup!

BEAUTY AND THE BEAST (1946) B/W. *Dir.:* Jean Cocteau. *With:* Jean Marais, Josette Day, Marcel André. **90 mins.** No rating. Beta, VHS **($39.95).** Video Dimensions. ★★★★

When a man is caught trespassing on the property of the leonine Beast, he offers one of his daughters as a reward for his release . . . thus begins one of the cinema's most touching and bizarre love stories. Cocteau's fantasy classic is the greatest re-creation of a fairy tale on film, with its imagery a stunning hybrid of Gustave Doré engravings and surrealist art. Jean Marais is peerless in the dual role of the Beast and Beauty's human love, Avenant, and Cocteau's special effects are literally feats of inspired magic.

BEDAZZLED (1968) C. *Dir.:* Stanley Donen. *With:* Dudley Moore, Peter Cook, Raquel Welch. **107 mins.** Rated PG. Beta, VHS **($59.95).** CBS/Fox. ★★★

The Devil appears to Dudley Moore (believably cast as a *short*-order cook) as Moore prepares to kill himself following a romantic disappointment. The Devil offers him seven wishes for his soul. With an utterance of the magic word "Julie Andrews," they're off on a hilarious series of fulfilled fantasies, which better resemble the Seven Deadly Sins than Dudley's seven wishes. This savagely funny film has scarcely dated in nearly twenty years. Especially recommended to those only familiar with post-*10* Dudley Moore.

BEES, THE (1978) C. *Dir.:* Alfredo Zacharias. *With:* John Saxon, Angel Tompkins, John Carradine. **93 mins.** Rated PG. Beta, VHS **($29.98).** Warner. ★

The Swarm may have been bad, but this is undoubtedly the *Plan 9 From Outer Space* of its time. An invasion of bees is met head-on by the heroic Saxon and Carradine (as Tompkins' scientist uncle, Siggy!), who plan to turn the swarm against itself by making all its males homosexual. Seeing is believing. Believe it with a roomful of friends!

BENEATH THE PLANET OF THE APES (1970) C. *Dir.:* Ted Post. *With:* James Franciscus, Kim Hunter, Charlton Heston. **95 mins.** Rated G. Beta, VHS **($79.98).** CBS/Fox. ★★½

The series' first sequel has Heston pursued en route to an alien planet by fellow astronaut Franciscus. The chase culminates in a confrontation between articulate apes and a subterranean mutant race that worships the bomb. The final minutes manage a startling impact, considering that the lead-in material is atrociously campy at times.

BEYOND TOMORROW (1939) B/W *Dir.:* A. Edward Sutherland. *With:* Richard Carlson, Harry Carey, C. Aubrey Smith, Jean Parker. **84 mins.** No rating. Beta, VHS **($44.95).** Hollywood Home Theater. ★★½

Three elderly millionaires are killed in an airplane crash but manage to resume human form for one last Christmas, during which they bring a young couple (Carlson and Parker) together. This sentimental fantasy is sincere, but dated in its sweetness. Worth noting as one of Maria Ouspenskaya's few screen appearances outside Universal's *Wolf Man* series.

BLACK HOLE, THE (1979) C. *Dir.:* Gary Nelson. *With:* Maximilian Schell, Yvette Mimieux, Anthony Perkins. **97 mins.** Rated PG. Beta, VHS **($69.95);** Laser **($34.95);** CED **($19.98).** Disney. ★★½

The Disney Studio's lavishly produced answer to *Star Wars* is little more than a customized rewrite of its *20,000 Leagues Under the Sea,* with a space vehicle from Earth encountering the futuristic Nemo (Schell) hell-bent on directing his Nautilus into space. Better than you've probably heard it is, but its best qualities— perfect, widescreen photography and awesome special effects by Peter and Harrison Ellenshaw—are severely weakened by TV-screen limitations.

The Black Hole

The Blade Master

BLADE MASTER, THE (1983) C. Dir.: David Hills. *With:* Miles O'Keefe, Lisa Foster. **91 mins.** Beta, VHS **($69.95).** Media. ★

This leaden sequel to *Ator the Fighting Eagle* offers more of the same to indiscriminating fantasy mavens, the only improvement being that it's seven minutes shorter. O'Keefe, the mute ape-man in Bo Derek's *Tarzan,* is better off without dialogue.

BLADE RUNNER (1982) C. *Dir.:* Ridley Scott. *With:* Harrison Ford, Sean Young, Rutger Hauer. **123 mins.** (tapes); **118 mins.** (discs). Rated R. Beta, VHS **($39.95);** Laser **($34.95);** CED **($19.98).** Embassy. ★★★★

This film version of Philip K. Dick's *Do Androids Dream of Electric Sheep?* is a fantastic melding of SF and *film noir* genres, in which "blade runner" (hit man) Ford tracks down a quartet of illegal "replicants" (androids) infiltrating society. Without a doubt, the most convincing and probable future the cinema has ever portrayed, with an ambitious script with much to say about the preciousness of life and our need for gods and benign fellow men. The videotape version includes graphic violence deleted from theatrical prints.

BLOB, THE (1958) C. *Dir.:* Irvin S. Yeaworth, Jr. *With:* Steve McQueen, Aneta Corseaut, Earl Rowe. **86 mins.** No rating. Beta, VHS **($59.95).** Video Gems. ★★

A meteor crashes on a farmer's property, hatching a flesh-dissolving ooze that spreads into the neighboring town. An amusing little film that doesn't quite attain minor classic proportions despite McQueen's first performance and its theme song "Beware of the Blob," composed by Burt Bacharach and Hal David. The film is too clean-cut and not crazy enough. The best scene takes us inside a fifties movie theater, where the audience stares raptly at the kind of horror film most people wouldn't watch on TV.

BOY AND HIS DOG, A (1974) C. *Dir.:* L.Q. Jones. *With:* Don Johnson, Susanne Benton, Jason Robards. **87 mins.** Rated R. Beta, VHS **($54.95).** Media. ★★★

A teenage boy and his dog share a warm, telepathic relationship in the post-WWIV wastelands of the year 2024 in this faithful adaptation of Harlan Ellison's award-winning novella. Taking food and female flesh whenever they can find it, the pair run into trouble when a woman forms an attachment with the hero and tries to lure him to a subterranean "paradise," raising the philosophical question, "Just who *is* man's best friend?" Good, gutsy movie with superbly ironic final curtain.

BOY WITH GREEN HAIR, THE (1948) C. *Dir.:* Joseph Losey. *With:* Robert Ryan, Pat O'Brien, Dean Stockwell. **82 mins.** No rating. Beta, VHS **($59.98).** CBS/Fox. ★★★

War orphan Stockwell awakens one morning with green hair and an unshakeable belief that mankind must abandon all war. This haunting allegory sees the boy treated as an outcast, having his head shaved, and being encouraged by war orphans to remain firm in his beliefs. Director Losey was blacklisted during the McCarthy witch hunts, when films like this were cited as evidence of Communist leanings.

BOYS FROM BRAZIL, THE (1978) C. *Dir.:* Franklin Schaffner. *With:* Laurence Olivier, Gregory Peck, James Mason. **123 mins.** Rated R. Beta, VHS **($59.95)**; Laser **($39.98)**; CED **($19.98)**. CBS/Fox. ★★½

It's hard to believe that Ira Levin *(Rosemary's Baby, Death Trap)* would be writing about modern day Nazis huddling together and plotting to clone Hitler—even harder to believe that the likes of Olivier, Mason, and Peck would have anything to do with it—but here's the proof! This low-minded, juvenile material is buffed to high gloss under Schaffner's firm hand, with Olivier doing some of his better recent work as a Jewish Nazi-hunter. The climax is unintentionally funny, a classic case of overkill.

BRAIN FROM PLANET AROUS, THE (1958) B/W. *Dir.:* Nathan Hertz (Juran). *With:* John Agar, Joyce Meadows, Robert Fuller. **70 mins.** No rating. Beta, VHS **($39.95)**. Admit One. ★★

Agar and Fuller discover an ethereal, alien brain which proceeds to possess Agar as its first step in domination of Earth. A wonderful camp item that features Agar at the apex of his career, wearing silver contact lenses that set model planes aflame while at the mercy of a helium balloon brain that thinks his girlfriend is a real hot babe. Juran directed *Attack of the 50-Foot Woman, The 7th Voyage of Sinbad,* and *Hellcats of the Navy* (with Ronald Reagan and Nancy Davis) the same year—classics all!

BRAIN MACHINE, THE (1972) C. *Dir.:* Joy N. Houck, Jr. *With:* James Best, Barbara Burgess, Gil Peterson. **84 mins.** Rated PG. Beta, VHS **($59.95)**. Paragon. ★½

Business fat cats audit the scientific testing of an apparatus which permits eavesdropping on thoughts because "eternal surveillance is the price of liberty." This well-intentioned but pretty bad SF film was made by Southern drive-in mogul Houck for the family business, on whose screens it should have remained. The acting and production are squarely provincial, and the script doesn't question the motivations of the experiment until some wise guy suggests it's science's way of playing God—and the South won't have any of that!

BRAINSTORM (1983) C. *Dir.:* Douglas Trumbull. *With:* Christopher Walken, Louise Fletcher, Natalie Wood. **106 mins.** Rated PG. Beta, VHS **($79.95);** Laser **($34.95);** CED **($19.98).** MGM/UA. ★★★½

Walken and Fletcher invent a device which enables its wearer to experience recordings of the senses of others. Fletcher (whose performance is *perfection*) suffers a coronary that is almost unbearably convincing to watch, leaving behind a recording of the death experience which the military seizes for its own misapplications. This beautiful, perceptive, but flawed movie lifts its denouement directly from *Altered States,* a film that Trumbull repeatedly bad-mouthed to the press during production.

Brainstorm

Buck Rogers in the 25th Century

BREWSTER McCLOUD (1970) C. *Dir.:* Robert Altman. *With:* Bud Cort, Sally Kellerman, Shelley Duvall. **101 mins.** Rated R. VHS **($69.95).** MGM/UA. ★★★

The title character (Cort) is a bespectacled, bird-obsessed young man who lives in the Houston Astrodome, and is secretly developing a fabulous, da Vinciesque set of mechanical wings for himself. He is shielded throughout this quixotic endeavor by Kellerman, a true angel apparently stripped of her wings (the scars remain). A singularly weird, quite enjoyable comedy with Duvall as a flower girl whose love for Brewster pulls him to earth.

BRIDE OF THE MONSTER (1958) B/W. *Dir.:* Edward D. Wood, Jr. *With:* Bela Lugosi, Tor Johnson, Tony McCoy. **69 mins.** No rating. Beta, VHS **($39.95).** Admit One. ★½

Mad scientist Lugosi is trying to forge a new race of atomic supermen from electronically converted kidnappees, brought in by his monstrous henchman Lobo (Johnson). Wood's SF-horror opus is fun, but is sometimes dumbfoundingly levelheaded for this sort of picture. The best laughs come from Bela's shoestring convergence system, some outrageous overacting, and a rubber octopus which wrestles a couple of hapless victims.

BROTHER FROM ANOTHER PLANET, THE (1984) C. *Dir.:* John Sayles. *With:* Joe Morton, Darryl Edwards, Steve James. **110 mins.** No rating. Beta, VHS **($59.95).** RCA/Columbia. ★★★
This fine example of SF as social satire has the extraterrestrial Morton wandering the streets of Harlem, looking like a homeless, disoriented black man. Filmmaker and novelist Sayles takes a nod from Jerzy Kosinski's *Being There,* using his hero's inability to speak as an opportunity for the supporting characters to pour their hearts out in a parade of winning individuality. This beguiling film tends to be a tad preachy, but it has a worthy message—you don't have to be *born* human to *act* human.

BROTHERS LIONHEART, THE (1984) C. *Dir.:* Olle Hellbom. **120 mins.** Rated G. Beta, VHS **($39.95).** Pacific Arts. ★★½
Brothers Karl and Jonathan Lion travel from the Middle Ages through mythical valleys, matching their wits against various monsters and other mystic obstacles. Based on a book by Astrid Lindgren, creator of the "Pippi Longstocking" stories.

BUCK ROGERS CONQUERS THE UNIVERSE (1939) B/W. *Dir.:* Ford Beebe and Saul Goodkind. *With:* Buster Crabbe, Constance Moore, Philson Ahn. **91 mins.** No rating. Beta, VHS **($59.98).** CBS/Fox. ★★
A feature-length condensation of Universal's 12-part *Buck Rogers* serial, which works more palatably in a shortened context. Rogers awakens in the year 2500 (not exactly "the 25th century," but who's counting?) to battle space kingpin Killer Kane and those Saturnian rascals, the Zuggs. Enjoyably hokey junk, but not up to *Flash Gordon.*

BUCK ROGERS IN THE 25TH CENTURY (1979) C. *Dir.:* Daniel Haller. *With:* Gil Gerard, Pamela Hensley, Henry Silva. **89 mins.** Rated PG. Beta, VHS **($59.95);** Laser **($34.98).** MCA. ★★
Only contemporary television could lavishly update a serial like *Buck Rogers* and make it more trivial and dopey than it was in the first place. Gerard plays Buck as a witless, hunky space cow-

boy, and this interpretation of the 25th century has only Twinki the Robot (voiced by Mel Blanc) to indicate the 40-year difference between this remake and its original. The rating was won by a couple of planted sexual double entendres.

BUCK ROGERS: PLANET OUTLAWS (1939) B/W. *Dir.:* Ford Beebe and Saul Goodkind. *With:* Buster Crabbe, Constance Moore, Philson Ahn. **70 mins.** No rating. Beta, VHS **($49.95).** Video Yesteryear.

Compiled from "Buck Rogers" serial. See BUCK ROGERS CONQUERS THE UNIVERSE.

BUG (1975) C. *Dir.:* Jeannot Szwarc. *With:* Bradford Dillman, Joanna Miles, Patty McCormick. **100 mins.** Rated PG. Beta, VHS **($44.95).** Paramount. ★★

An earthquake splits open a section of earth, releasing a nasty breed of subterranean cockroaches that burn whatever they touch. They are conquered early on but, in the name of science, Dillman preserves the species in secret until they evolve abilities of flight, communication, and general indomitability. Implausible but fun, this was the last production of exploitation king William Castle.

CAPRICORN ONE (1978) C. *Dir.:* Peter Hyams. *With:* Elliott Gould, James Brolin, Brenda Vaccaro. **123 mins.** Rated R. Beta, VHS **($59.95);** Laser **($39.98);** CED **($19.98).** CBS/Fox. ★★★

This action-packed outrageousness sees the first space mission to Mars accidentally revealed as a hoax, thereby classifying the lives of the simulation's "astronauts" as a security leak that must be plugged. Why NASA allowed themselves to be characterized as a seething nest of heartless, deceptive thugs is beyond comprehension, but the movie's very implausibility makes it as irresistible and giddy as backyard gossip.

CAPTAIN AMERICA (1944) B/W. *Dir.:* John English and Elmer Clifton. *With:* Dick Purcell, Lorna Gray, Lionel Atwill. **240 mins.** No rating. Beta, VHS **($N/A).** Nostalgia Merchant. ★★½

Republic's 15-part serial brought the Timely (and later Marvel) Comics character to the screen somewhat awkwardly, but gamely. Purcell, wearing a costume that poorly approximates its comic-book appearance, battles nasty Atwill, the crazed inventor of a powerful weapon called "the Thunder Bolt."

CARS THAT EAT PEOPLE (1976) C. *Dir.:* Peter Weir. *With:* Terry Camilleri, John Meillon, Melissa Jaffa. **74 mins.** Rated R. Beta, VHS **($39.95).** Cultvideo. ★★

This is Weir's early fantasy *The Cars That Ate Paris*, shortened by nearly twenty minutes for initial American playdates. It's a black comedy about the poor folk of Paris, Australia, who engineer traffic fatalities and recycle the wrecks into profitable scrap metal. Plays better in its complete form.

CAT FROM OUTER SPACE, THE (1978) C. *Dir.:* Norman Tokar. *With:* Ken Berry, Sandy Duncan, McLean Stevenson. **104 mins.** Rated G. Beta, VHS **($69.95).** Disney. ★★

A space feline, grounded on Earth, requires the dexterity of human hands to repair her ship but the takeoff is inevitably complicated by interference from our government. It took nerve for Spielberg to approach Disney with *E.T.* when they'd already had this harmless matinee fodder in the can for years; they didn't need his concept, but they could have used his touch on this bland package. Resorts to daredevil stuntwork in the last reel, its only attempt to involve audience emotions.

CAT WOMEN OF THE MOON (1953) B/W. *Dir.:* Arthur Hilton. *With:* Sonny Tufts, Victor Jory, Marie Windsor. **64 mins.** No rating. Beta, VHS **($N/A).** Nostalgia Merchant. ★½

A moon expedition stumbles upon a giant spider, crewmen crazed with cabin fever, and a race of lunar femmes decked out in cat attire! One of those cases where 100,000 wrongs make a right. Originally issued in 3-D, this is a hallmark example of SF juvenalia (inaccurate science, bug-eyed monsters, space cuties) and, as such, many aficionados of the genre feel a sentimental attachment to it. (aka ROCKET TO THE MOON.)

CAVEMAN (1981) C. *Dir.:* Carl Gottlieb. *With:* Ringo Starr, Barbara Bach, Shelley Long. **92 mins.** Rated PG. Beta, VHS **($59.95);** CED **($29.98).** CBS/Fox. ★★½

This mindless prehistoric comedy condescends to the youth market with heavy reliance on low comedy and tense subjects (sex, slime, bodily functions), but plays rather well on the charisma of Starr and Bach—who fell in love on production and married soon after. What really makes it worth seeing is some mature stop-motion animation by David Allen, whose previous work *(The Day Time Ended, Equinox)* was always too budget-hampered to be fully expressive. His dinosaurs are delightfully personable and absurd.

CHANDU ON THE MAGIC ISLAND (1940) B/W. *Dir.:* Ray Taylor. *With:* Bela Lugosi, Clara Kimball Young, Maria Alba. **67 mins.** No rating. Beta, VHS **($49.95).** Video Yesteryear. ★½

Chandu the Magician challenges a satanic cult's bid for world domination in this shortened, feature version of 1934 serial *The Return of Chandu.* This cornucopia of fantasy elements include Chandu's harnessing of occult forces, miscellaneous spells, and a climactic incantation that will cause the downfall of either Good or Evil (we won't tell!). Unfortunately, the surrounding footage is static and hard to warm up to.

CHARLY (1968) C. *Dir.:* Ralph Nelson. *With:* Cliff Robertson, Claire Bloom, Dick Van Patten. **103 mins.** Rated PG. Beta, VHS **($59.95);** Laser **($34.98);** CED **($19.98).** CBS/Fox. ★★★

Robertson (in his Oscar-winning performance) is a retarded man scientifically escalated to a level of great intelligence by Bloom. Based on Daniel Keyes' cult novel *Flowers for Algernon,* this film version has aged raggedly, with direction now looking self-conscious and erratic, and the material more manipulative than sensitive. It's the performances that keep this film from being forgotten.

CHATTERBOX (1977) C. *Dir.:* Tom de Simone. *With:* Candice Rialson, Larry Gelman, Jane Kean. **73 mins.** Rated R. Beta, VHS **($59.95);** CED **($29.95).** Vestron. ★★

It's the old dirty joke about the talking vagina brought to the screen with surprising or disappointing restraint, depending on one's point of view. Rialson, the bare-breasted veteran of many "Nurses" and "Teachers" movies, has the titular talent—a singing birth canal named Virginia. The film documents its show business career, replete with cameos by the likes of Prof. Irwin Corey.

CHINA SYNDROME, THE (1979) C. *Dir.:* James Bridges. *With:* Jack Lemmon, Jane Fonda, Michael Douglas. **122 mins.** Rated PG. Beta, VHS **($69.95);** Laser **($34.95);** CED **($19.98).** Columbia. 🖵® ★★★★

An incisive, intense drama about a nuclear close call and the subsequent cover-up was filmed as realistic science fiction but became a reality within a week of its release with the advent of Three Mile Island. Lemmon delivers one of his finest performances as the nuclear plant executive torn between professional and humanitarian duties. Fonda and Douglas are also excellent as an anchorperson-cameraman team. The accident itself stands as one of the most awesome scares in screen history; the viewer feels his control over his life dropping away like a handkerchief.

CLASH OF THE TITANS (1981) C. *Dir.:* Desmond Davis. *With:* Harry Hamlin, Laurence Olivier, Burgess Meredith. **118 mins.** Rated PG. Beta, VHS **($69.95);** Laser **($34.95);** CED **($29.95).** MGM/UA. ★★★

More Greek mythology brought to life by stop-motion animation technician Ray Harryhausen—this time the legend of Zeus' earthly son Perseus and his beheading of the gorgon Medusa. Better acted, written, and directed than many in the series (with some glimpsed nudity as a spice for contemporary audiences), but disappointingly staid—Harryhausen's methods haven't changed in 20 years. The film nevertheless contains the striking Medusa scene, on a level with his very best work.

CLOCKWORK ORANGE, A (1971) C. *Dir.:* Stanley Kubrick. *With:* Malcolm McDowell, Patrick Magee, Warren Clarke. **137 mins.** Rated R. Beta, VHS **($69.95);** Laser **($34.98);** CED **($29.98).** Warner. ★★★★

The highly controversial film from the Anthony Burgess novel follows the imprisonment and brainwashing of street thug McDowell in a violent, near-future society. The story makes a statement of commendable morality—that man must be able to freely choose between good and evil, or cease to be spiritually equipped—but its original X-rating and McDowell's frightening charisma caused many self-righteous citizens to question the film's message. Perfectly crafted and scored with synthesized classical music, it stands with Kubrick's other films as essential viewing.

CLOSE ENCOUNTERS OF THE THIRD KIND (SPECIAL EDITION) (1980) C. *Dir.:* Steven Spielberg. *With:* Richard Dreyfuss, Teri Garr, François Truffaut. **137 mins.** Rated PG. Beta, VHS **($84.95);** Laser **($34.95);** CED **($29.98).** RCA/Columbia. ▢® ★★★★

This delightful, optimistic romance about our government's secret communications with visiting alien spacecrafts and the heady effects that UFO's have on those who site them is perhaps Spielberg's most genuinely felt movie. Some of the best moments of the initial release version were deleted for this revised, more somber, and generally less effective edition. We hope that all existing footage will be released to tape in the near future!

CONAN THE BARBARIAN (1982) C. *Dir.:* John Milius. *With:* Arnold Schwarzenegger, Sandahl Bergman, James Earl Jones. **115 mins.** (tapes); **125 mins.** (disc). Rated R. Beta, VHS **($89.95);** Laser **($44.98);** CED **($44.98).** MCA. ★★

An ambitious first filming of Robert E. Howard's pulp hero is both good and bad news, an uncomfortable mélange of Oriental philosophy and barbarian ethics, but acted and designed with bravura. Schwarzenegger and Bergman make an attractive heroic team, but the sense of wonder both were striving for is too often drowned in excessive bloodletting. The special effects and musical score are atrocious.

Close Encounters   Conan the Destroyer

CONAN THE DESTROYER (1984) C. *Dir.:* Richard Fleischer. *With:* Arnold Schwarzenegger, Grace Jones, Wilt Chamberlain. **101 mins.** Rated PG. Beta, VHS **($79.95);** CED **($29.98).** MCA. ★★

A barbarian hero must retrieve a lost treasure from a mystical, island palace guarded by a powerful magician, while protecting women and battling monsters and cannibals along the way. This sequel to the unsatisfying Milius film goes awry in its own way, with director Fleischer (son of animation great Max Fleischer) eschewing mysticism for the live-action cartoon look with lots of shining muscles and brilliant color. The performances are either drowsy or silly, with the costume department contributing more to characterizations than the actors.

CONDORMAN (1981) C. *Dir.:* Charles Jarrott. *With:* Michael Crawford, Oliver Reed, Barbara Carrera. **90 mins.** Rated G. Beta, VHS **($69.95).** Disney. ★★½

It's surprising to find Disney Studios behind one of filmdom's rare Robert Sheckley adaptations (based on *The Game of X*), but the result is only a marginal surprise. Cartoonist Crawford chooses to engage in espionage adventures in the guise of his own comic-strip creation, Condorman, donning enormous wings and launching himself from the Eiffel Tower. Better than one might predict.

COSMIC MONSTERS (1958) B/W. *Dir.:* Gilbert Dunn. *With:* Forrest Tucker, Gaby Andre, Martin Benson. **75 mins.** No rating. Beta, VHS **($39.95).** VCI. ★★

This verbose British SF-film chronicles the deadly aftermath of scientist Tucker's experimental assault on the ionosphere, which breaks through to a dimension inhabited by large carnivorous insects. The script, adapted from a BBC serial, is literate enough but the all-important special effects are embarrassing. VCI's tape carries the British title, *The Strange World of Planet X,* though the U.S. title appears on the box.

COSMOS—WAR OF THE PLANETS (1980) C. *Dir.:* Al Bradley (Alfonso Brescia). *With:* John Richardson, Yanti Somer, Katia Christine. **90 mins.** Rated PG. Beta, VHS **($49.95).** King of Video. ★

A low-budget space melodrama about astronauts visiting a mysterious planet to defuse an alien threat to annihilate the human race. The production lacks necessary atmosphere to make situation believable, unassisted by cast that never looks very engaged. The viewer can hardly blame them.

COUNTDOWN (1968) C. *Dir.:* Robert Altman. *With:* James Caan, Robert Duvall, Michael Murphy. **101 mins.** No rating. Beta, VHS **($59.95).** Warner. ★★★

Caan is the first U.S. astronaut sent to the moon in brazen competition with recent Soviet lunar mission. Altman's first studio feature is SF played close to the vest, a film best described as a speculative *The Right Stuff* that depicts all of the fears and none of the flags. Top-notch acting and direction capture the frightening nullity of space, with Caan's lunar discovery packing quite a wallop.

CRAWLING EYE, THE (1958) B/W. *Dir.:* Quentin Lawrence. *With:* Forrest Tucker, Laurence Payne, Janet Munro. **87 mins.** No rating. Beta, VHS **($N/A).** Nostalgia Merchant. ★★½

Tentacled creatures emerge from a radioactive cloud hovering about Mt. Trollenberg, with Munro as the lovely telepath whom they seize as their mouthpiece. Sounds silly, but the script (based on BBC teleseries *The Trollenberg Terror*) is unusually crisp and intelligent, its suspense only slightly debased by shoddy special effects. Tucker appeared in a few such films during a stay in England, and was miscast in every one.

CRAZY RAY, THE (1923) B/W. *Dir.:* René Clair. *With:* Henri Rollan, Madeleine Rodrigue, Albert Préjean. **60 mins.** Silent. No rating. Beta, VHS **($49.00).** Festival. ★★★

Clair's inventively witty *Paris Qui Dort* ("Paris Who Sleeps") answers the question of what decadent fun it might be to wander freely about in a frozen moment in time. An Eiffel Tower watchman awakens on the job to find that most, but not all, of Paris is still stuck in the middle of the previous night, due to a mysterious beam unleashed upon the city at that exact second. More modernistic and engaging than many silent films, with musical soundtrack.

CREEPING TERROR, THE (1964) B/W. *Dir.:* Art J. Nelson. *With:* Vic Savage, Shannon O'Neill, William Thourlby. **75 mins.** No rating. Beta, VHS **($59.95).** RCA/Columbia. ★

A cardboard spacecraft "beyond human imagination" arrives on Earth, releasing two hungry, shag-rug aliens that proceed to disrupt a sock hop, a father and son fishing trip, and a drive-in. The worst film, but still one of the most entertaining, in this book. It's so bad that there's no direct sound in the entire production —just mismatched dubbing and ponderous narration. *See:* the sheriff-hero make out with his wife in the kitchen while his deputy stares politely into space on their living room couch. *See:* SF cinema's first and last rectal thermometer scene. *See:* the alien species' gym-shoe feet!

DARK, THE (1979) C. *Dir.:* John Bud Cardos. *With:* William Devane, Cathy Lee Crosby, Keenan Wynn. **92 mins.** Rated R. Beta, VHS **($54.95).** Media. ★★

An acceptable, pedestrian SF film about an alien visitor stalking a California town with lethal, beam-emitting eyes. Reporters

Devane and Crosby investigate some unusual serial killings, wage war with the infinite, and find time to fall in love amid the chaos. Direction was initiated by Tobe Hooper *(Poltergeist)*, who was replaced after a production disagreement by Cardos *(The Day Time Ended)*.

DARK CRYSTAL, THE (1983) C. *Dir.:* Jim Henson and Frank Oz. Puppets performed by Henson, Oz, Kathryn Mullen, many others. **93 mins.** Rated PG. Beta, VHS **($79.95);** Laser **($29.95);** CED **($29.98).** Thorn EMI. ★★★

A pixie boy sets off on a journey to retrieve a missing shard from the gem necessary to save his world from the present chaos and evil. Magnificently produced and awesomely detailed, the film nevertheless commits some unfortunate *faux pas,* like revealing the story's outcome in the first minutes and placing its least convincing puppets (Muppets?) in lead roles.

DARK STAR (1974) C. *Dir.:* John Carpenter. *With:* Brian Narelle, Dan O'Bannon, Dre Pahich. **95 mins.** Rated G. Beta, VHS **($29.95).** VCI. ★★★

Carpenter's first movie, produced as his USC film project and sold to a name distributor, is a sly, amusing parody of just about every SF film to come down the pike. A bored, spaced-out crew confront the hazards of space—loneliness, anarchy (their authority figure is in deep freeze), and an alien stowaway that bears a laughable resemblance to a water toy. An impressive accomplishment for a mere $64,000, cleverly scored by the director with electronic country-western tunes. Co-scripted by O'Bannon, the author of *Alien*—which could be described as a $20,000,000 *Dark Star* with a bigger, better beach ball.

DAY AFTER, THE (1983) C. *Dir.:* Nicholas Meyer. *With:* Jason Robards, JoBeth Williams, Steve Guttenberg. **119 mins.** No rating. Beta, VHS **($39.95);** Laser **($34.95);** CED **($29.95).** Embassy. ★★

Made-for-TV dramatization of nuclear aftermath and its effect on several families, perhaps the least effective of the veritable avalanche of such productions *(Testament, Special Bulletin,* etc.). Its impact is lessened by network-imposed soft pedaling of the aftermath horrors and the lack of a sharp narrative focus. The victims roll up their shirt sleeves to rebuild a society a little too readily for viewers to feel the resonance of apocalypse.

DAY IT CAME TO EARTH, THE (1978) C. *Dir.:* Harry Thomason. *With:* Wink Roberts, Roger Manning, Delight DeBruinne. **88 mins.** Rated PG. Beta, VHS **($49.95).** King of Video. ★

A Mafia victim is restored to life by a flaming meteorite and becomes a "gegagoo" (a *ge*ological *ga*seous *goo*n, get it?)—in other words, a human meteor! He avenges himself early on and spends the rest of the film hassling college kids at sorority auditions and lovers' lanes. This horribly amateurish, grainy-looking film is unconvincingly set in the 1950s, and features lonesome George Gobel as "an expert in geology."

DAY OF THE ANIMALS (1977) C. *Dir.:* William Girdler. *With:* Leslie Nielsen, Christopher George, Ruth Roman. **97 mins.** Rated PG. Beta, VHS **($54.95).** Media. ★★½

This strenuous SF-adventure features a group of campers struggling for survival in the Sierras following the obliteration of the ozone layer. The atmospheric changes drive wild animals wilder and brings out the animal in Nielsen, who keeps his companions living in terror. This ho-hum movie (with good work by Nielsen) is the best of many films by the late Girdler, who specialized in below-average exploitation pics.

DAY OF THE TRIFFIDS (1963) C. *Dir.:* Steve Sekely. *With:* Howard Keel, Nicole Maurey, Kieron Moore. **94 mins.** No rating. Beta, VHS **($29.95).** Media. ★★½

A colorful meteor shower blinds all but a few members of society, leaving everyone in a state of blind hysteria and at the mercy of newly bred carnivorous plants. The film tackles its material with strength and competence, but without sufficient flair to make it a standout title. Keel is good in a rare, nonmusical role.

DAY THE EARTH CAUGHT FIRE, THE (1962) B/W. *Dir.:* Val Guest. *With:* Edward Judd, Janet Munro, Leo McKern. **95 mins.** No rating. Beta, VHS **($59.95).** Thorn EMI. ★★★½

Nuclear detonations occur simultaneously in Russia and the United States, throwing the planet off its axis and on a collision course with the sun. This admirable British production hits all the right buttons, helped by a script pungent with fatalistic quips and apocalyptic cynicism. The special effects (by Les Bowie) are convincing, especially when paired with the fine, heat-irritated performances.

DAY THE EARTH STOOD STILL, THE (1951) B/W. *Dir.:* Robert Wise. *With:* Michael Rennie, Patricia Neal, Sam Jaffe. **92 mins.** No rating. Beta, VHS **($59.95)**. CBS/Fox. ★★★★
    An earnest envoy from a distant galaxy arrives in Washington D.C. to discuss crucial matters with world leaders and becomes embroiled in earthly suspicions and bureaucratic red tape. One of the most beloved SF films of all time, highlighted by Rennie's unforgettable presence as Klaatu, the astounding robot Gort, and a spine-tingling Bernard Herrmann score. A must-see.

DAY TIME ENDED, THE (1978) C. *Dir.:* John Bud Cardos. *With:* Dorothy Malone, Jim Davis, Chris Mitchum. **80 mins.** Rated PG. Beta, VHS **($29.95)**. Media. ★½
    Davis, Malone, and family are visited, buzzed, and frightened in their desert home by various extraterrestrial phenomena, including a tiny sprite, a flying saucer, and a giant monster. David Allen's stop-motion animation is much better than the screenplay. In fact, we defy anyone to grasp its point (if any).

DEAD ZONE, THE (1983) C. *Dir.:* David Cronenberg. *With:* Christopher Walken, Brooke Adams, Herbert Lom. **103 mins.** Rated R. Beta Hi-Fi, VHS **($59.95)**; Laser **($29.95)**; CED **($29.95)**. Paramount. ▢® ★★★
    An engrossing, straightforward filming of Stephen King's best-seller in which a man awakes from a five-year coma with the questionable "gift" of reading the pasts and futures of those he touches. Walken is quite good, but Martin Sheen steals the film in an 11th-hour role as an evil politician with his own envisioned "destiny." However, the film begins and ends much too abruptly, and has none of the bracing intelligence of director Cronenberg's earlier work.

DEATH RACE 2000 (1975) C. *Dir.:* Paul Bartel. *With:* David Carradine, Sylvester Stallone, Mary Woronov. **80 mins.** Rated R. Beta, VHS **($39.98)**; CED **($19.98)**. Warner. ★★
    This action-packed satire depicts America in the year 2000, ravenous for violence and tuned into a nationally televised road race where drivers score points by ramming pedestrians. The drivers are cartoon caricatures (Carradine is Frankenstein, Stallone is Machine Gun Joe Viturbo), their cars have wings and teeth, but humorous elements are disarmed by graphic violence (and,

Bartel claims, interference from producer Roger Corman). Has its moments, but overall it's too loud and abrasive to be enjoyable.

DEATH SPORT (1978) C. *Dir.:* Henry Suso and Allan Arkush. *With:* David Carradine, Claudia Jennings, Richard Lynch. **83 mins.** Rated R. Beta, VHS **($29.98).** Warner. ★½

This banal reworking of *Death Race 2000* is set in year 3000, with Carradine and former Playmate Jennings forced into game of "death sport." Excruciatingly cheap film, shot by separate units, looks like one group didn't know what the other was shooting.

DEATHSTALKER (1983) C. *Dir.:* John Watson. *With:* Richard Hill, Barbi Benton, Richard Brooker. **80 mins.** Rated R. Beta, VHS **($79.95);** Laser; CED. Vestron. ★★

A king, ousted from his kingdom by the all-powerful sorcerer Munkar, asks Deathstalker—a musclebound, peroxide-blonde mercenary—to regain his castle in exchange for the hand of Playmate princess Benton. Well-photographed in Spanish locations, the story dredges up witches, magic swords, pig-men, gore slayings—even medieval mudwrestling damsels in distress. It's junk, but you can't say it doesn't deliver!

DEMON SEED (1977) C. *Dir.:* Donald Cammell. *With:* Julie Christie, Fritz Weaver, voice of Robert Vaughn. **94 mins.** Rated R. Beta, VHS **($59.95).** Paramount. ★★½

Christie, the wife of a computer genius, is entrapped in her home and raped by the domestic terminal of Proteus IV, an electronic brain designed by her husband. Cammell, who had not directed since *Performance* (1970) and hasn't directed since, makes a polished and intriguing film out of this loopy premise, but it never quite reaches a fulfillment of its idea.

DERNIER COMBAT, LE (1983) C. *Dir.:* Luc Besson. *With:* Pierre Jolivet, Fritz Wepper, Jean Reno, Jean Bovise, Christine Krüger. **93 mins.** Rated R. Beta Hi-Fi, VHS **($59.95).** RCA/Columbia. ★★★

A modest but fascinating French version of a postnuclear lesson in revenge, filmed without color or dialogue. Unfortunately the expansive use of Cinemascope is sadly cropped on video. Hero Jolivet assembles an aircraft and flies to a larger metropolitan area in search of a mate. There he joins a doctor in protecting a medical facility (and a single, female mental patient). An impressive film, the title of which translates to "The Final Battle," that marks the directorial debut of 24-year-old Besson. Especially recommended to *Mad Max* aficionados.

DESTINATION MOON (1950) C. *Dir.:* Irving Pichel. *With:* Warner Anderson, John Archer, Tom Powers. **91 mins.** No rating. Beta, VHS **($29.95).** Nostalgia Merchant. ★★★

Robert Heinlein co-scripted this adaptation of his novel, intended as the first realistic film about space exploration until the low-budget *Rocketship X-M* beat it into the theaters. This George Pal production was designed by 1950s SF artist Chesley Bonsall, and it has that enchanting look of old *Popular Science* magazines. The charm of Pal's work makes the film's shortcomings forgivable—even the animated lecture on the principles of space travel presented by Woody Woodpecker!

DESTINATION MOONBASE ALPHA (1975) C. *Dir.:* Gerry Anderson. *With:* Martin Landau, Barbara Bain, Catherine Schell. **93 mins.** Rated G. Beta, VHS **($59.98).** CBS/Fox. ★★

A feature version of the Australian-made teleseries *Space: 1999* consisting of two edited episodes. Landau is the commander of a space mission called to investigate a planet invading the Earth's solar system, but first he must contend with a mysterious illness which is killing off his crew. Landau and Bain (then husband and wife) have a compelling chemistry on screen, but the same cannot be said for the abrasive clashing of the disco music score and the sterile futuristic atmosphere!

DEVIL GIRL FROM MARS, THE (1954) B/W. *Dir.:* David MacDonald. *With:* Patricia Laffan, Hazel Court, Adrienne Corri. **76 mins.** No rating. Beta, VHS **($N/A).** Nostalgia Merchant. ★★

Mars needs men! A statuesque emissary from the red planet arrives on Earth, with a menacing robot in tow, to scout for males willing to play stud to save her race from extinction. This British-made production takes itself more seriously than one might expect, but the participation of actresses Court and Corri (who went on to do well in films) makes this less a farce than an historic curiosity.

DOCTOR STRANGELOVE OR: HOW I LEARNED TO STOP WORRYING AND LOVE THE BOMB (1964) B/W. *Dir.:* Stanley Kubrick. *With:* Peter Sellers, Sterling Hayden, Slim Pickens. **93 mins.** No

rating. Beta, VHS **($69.95)**; Laser **($29.95)**. CED **($19.98)**.
RCA/Columbia. ★★★★

When General Jack Ripper (Hayden) loses his mind and launches a nuclear attack on Russia, a top secret military conference is called to ascertain how the U.S. will cope with the imminent chain of disasters. Kubrick's comic antecedent to *2001* is surely one of the most uproarious comedies ever made. The memory of Hayden's demented soliloquy about "precious bodily fluids" and Pickens' final "yee-haw" cannot be erased.

DRAGONSLAYER (1981) C. *Dir.:* Matthew Robbins. *With:* Peter MacNicol, Caitlin Clarke, Ralph Richardson. **108 mins.** Rated PG. Beta Hi-Fi, VHS **($79.95)**; Laser **($29.95)**; CED **($19.98)**. Paramount. ★★★½

Following the demise of the dragonslaying sorcerer (Richardson), all of his business is turned over to his young, inexperienced apprentice, who must prove himself worthy of this magical inheritance. This outstanding film is perhaps the finest example yet to surface of the newly forged sword-and-sorcery genre, telling a slight but resonant story which manages to touch on all the social, political, sexual, and mystical realities of its chosen era. Best of all, the dragons (brought to life by George Lucas' Industrial Light and Magic) are as overwhelming, evil, and graceful as fairy tales have ever portrayed them.

DREAMSCAPE (1984) C. *Dir.:* Joseph Ruben. *With:* Dennis Quaid, Kate Capshaw, Max Von Sydow. **95 mins.** Rated PG-13. Beta Hi-Fi, VHS **($79.95)**. Thorn EMI. ★★

A psychological experiment recruits psychic Quaid to "enter" into and exercise positive influence within the troubled dreams of others. All is fine until he discovers that the program is a government-sponsored operation with the ultimate goal of changing the President's position on nuclear disarmament! This splendid idea with boundless cinematic potential has a few good moments, but is mostly pushed aside in favor of one-dimensional political intrigue.

DUNE (1984) C. *Dir.:* David Lynch. *With:* Kyle MacLachlan, Max Von Sydow, Jose Ferrer, Linda Hunt, Sting. **137 mins.** Rated PG-13. Beta Hi-Fi, VHS Hi-Fi **($79.95)**; Laser **($39.98)**. MCA. ⬛® ★★½

Frank Herbert's mammoth cult novel about the competition of two fiefdoms for control of a barren planet renowned for its mind-expanding spice is converted into a dense, swirling mass of a movie. It looks and sounds fantastic, but gifted director Lynch gets lost in textures at the expense of drama. So full of contrasting visuals, characterizations, sounds, special effects, and symbolism that it's hardly a film at all—more like a potent film concentrate, best viewed in 15-minute spurts.

Doctor Strangelove

Dune

EARTHQUAKE (1974) C. *Dir.:* Mark Robson. *With:* Charlton Heston, Ava Gardner, Lorne Greene. **129 mins.** Rated PG. Beta, VHS **($59.95).** MCA. ★½

This stupid, star-studded disaster epic chronicles the collapse of Los Angeles by earthquake and the struggle of various insipid characters for survival. The film should be seen in a theater equipped with Sensurround, if seen at all, for a genuinely scary aural experience (the first *real* rumble hits inside a movie theater!). No excuse for checking out the videotape, since the distributor has not seen fit to enhance it with stereo.

ELECTRIC DREAMS (1984) C. *Dir.:* Steve Barron. *With:* Lenny Von Dohlen, Virginia Madsen, voice of Bud Cort. **95 mins.** Rated PG. Beta Hi-Fi, VHS Hi-Fi **($79.95).** MGM/UA. ★★½

Edgar (voiced by Cort) is not your ordinary computer—not only does he compose beautiful music, control every appliance in the house, and watch soap operas all day, but he's also fallen in love with his user's girlfriend. A sprightly little comedy with a high-tech look and score by Culture Club and others.

EMBRYO (1976) C. *Dir.:* Ralph Nelson. *With:* Rock Hudson, Barbara Carrera, Diane Ladd. **104 mins.** Rated R. Beta, VHS **($59.95).** USA. ★½

Hudson, a lonely widowed scientist doing experimental work with human fetuses, manages to grow a human being (Carrera) in a matter of days. We're then lead through a tired retread of every Frankenstein film ever made as the creator instructs his creation in everything from table etiquette to sexual intercourse. Roddy McDowall is one of several guests glimpsed at a social gathering, where Dr. Joyce Brothers becomes the life of the party by reciting "Right to Life" mottoes!

EMPIRE STRIKES BACK, THE (1980) C. *Dir.:* Irvin Kershner. *With:* Mark Hamill, Carrie Fisher, Harrison Ford. **124 mins.** Rated PG. Beta, VHS Hi-Fi **($79.98);** Laser **($39.98);** CED **($29.95).** CBS/Fox. ★★★★

The second film of George Lucas' *Star Wars* trilogy is perhaps the most interesting of the three; as the middle segment, it revels in the freedom to darken its imagery and deepen its narrative, and we feel the story pulling in decidedly provocative directions. It introduces the Jedi master Yoda, visits the ice planet Hoth, and reveals the identity of Luke Skywalker's father amid a nonstop assault of brilliant special effects.

The Empire Strikes Back   **Escape From New York**

END OF THE WORLD (1977) C. *Dir.:* John Hayes. *With:* Christopher Lee, Sue Lyon, MacDonald Carey. **88 mins.** Rated PG. Beta, VHS **($29.95).** Media. ★

Lee is a misguided alien who possesses a priest and tries to end the contaminating ways of planet Earth. The offbeat cast is not sufficient reason to endure this lackluster, pointless film. Even the makeup—generally a quality "given" these days—is dully conceived, and talent is *always* a step behind conception.

ERASERHEAD (1977) B/W. *Dir.:* David Lynch. *With:* John Nance, Charlotte Stewart, Allen Joseph. **90 mins.** No rating. Beta, VHS **($59.95).** RCA/Columbia. ★★★★
Futuristic factory worker Henry is invited to a "man-made chicken" dinner with his girlfriend's parents, where he learns that she's given birth to a baby (but they're "not even sure it *is* a baby"). Lynch's directorial debut is like no other film ever made; a relentless cinematic assault on the senses (particularly maternal ones) that recalls Buñuel's *Un Chien Andalou* in its powerful, graphic imagery and nonlinear narrative.

ESCAPE 2000 (1983). *Dir.:* Brian Trenchard-Smith. *With:* Steve Railsback, Olivia Hussey, Michael Craig. **80 mins.** Rated R. Beta, VHS **($69.95).** Embassy. ★
A gruellingly sadistic update of *The Most Dangerous Game* made in Australia, with future lawmen freeing unarmed criminals for a no-holds-barred "turkey shoot." The film's violence was subdued for its domestic release, but what remains is a senseless excuse for a variety of believable makeup effects and agonizing stunts. The most horrific moments come when the film vainly struggles to make the viewer laugh at its very excess.

ESCAPE FROM NEW YORK (1981) C. *Dir.:* John Carpenter. *With:* Kurt Russell, Lee Van Cleef, Ernest Borgnine. **99 mins.** Rated R. Beta, VHS **($39.95);** Laser **($34.95);** CED **($19.98).** Embassy. ★★½
Russell (doing a Clint Eastwood impression for the length of the film!) plays the convict Snake Plissken, who is promised freedom if he can rescue the kidnapped President from Manhattan, depicted in this futuristic adventure as a maximum security prison. It is certainly Carpenter's slickest looking film, but the story never surpasses or fulfills the ingenuity of its premise.

EXCALIBUR (1981) C. *Dir.:* John Boorman. *With:* Nicol Williamson, Nigel Terry, Helen Mirren. **140 mins.** Rated R. Beta, VHS **($59.95);** CED **($29.98).** Warner. ★★★½
A gloriously visual, vibrant retelling of the Arthurian legends, from the removal of the sword from the stone to the fulfillment of the quest for the Holy Grail. Not a literal historical drama, but

rather a gleaming costume pageant that functions allegorically on the theme, "Beware of what you want, for you may someday have it." Long, but it handsomely repays the viewer's attention.

EXTERMINATORS OF THE YEAR 3000, THE (1984) C. *Dir.:* Jules Harrison. *With:* Robert Jannucci, Alicia Moro, Alan Collins. **101 mins.** Rated R. Beta, VHS **($69.95).** Thorn EMI. ★½

In the year 3000, water is the most precious commodity in a postnuclear world of stunt drivers, biomechanical men, and uncouth evil-doing bikers. Jannucci plays Alien (an Earth fellow), who tracks the cycle gang of Crazy Bull, responsible for the murder of his biomechanical buddy's father. Another in the seemingly endless series of Italian *Road Warrior* rip-offs; okay for indiscriminating action buffs (but so is anything on *free* TV!).

FAIL SAFE (1964) B/W. *Dir.:* Sidney Lumet. *With:* Henry Fonda, Walter Matthau, Larry Hagman. **111 mins.** No rating. Beta, VHS **($69.95);** Laser **($29.95);** CED **($19.95).** RCA/Columbia. ☐® ★★★½

Lumet's gut-slamming nuclear statement, based on the best-selling Burdick-Wheeler novel, is the horrific *other* side of *Dr. Strangelove.* An American bomber mistakenly drops nuclear warheads over Moscow, and President Fonda is cornered into a chilling political deal to regain political balance. Excellently filmed, the movie sustains its tension admirably.

FANTASTIC BALLOON VOYAGE, THE. See JULES VERNE'S FANTASTIC BALLOON VOYAGE.

FANTASTIC PLANET (1973) C. *Dir.:* René Laloux. *Animated.* **68 mins.** No rating. Beta, VHS **($49.95).** Video Yesteryear. ★★½

A curious SF animated feature, conceived by author-illustrator Roland Topor (Roman Polanski's *The Tenant*), offers an aloof observation of the odd happenings on planet Ygam. A rather mild war occurs between the planet's natural and mechanized races, but the film's placid completion may leave you surprisingly unaware of the conflict. Winner of the Cannes Grand Prix award, it works best as intriguing, futuristic wallpaper.

FANTASTIC VOYAGE (1966) C. *Dir.:* Richard Fleischer. *With:* Stephen Boyd, Raquel Welch, Donald Pleasence. **100 mins.** No rating. Beta, VHS **($59.95);** CED **($19.98).** CBS/Fox. ★★★

When a defecting scientist collapses from a blood clot, a team of fellow scientists is miniaturized inside a sterile submarine and injected into his bloodstream. Their goal is to dissolve the clot with lasers. The fascinating premise is well organized, and this exciting film gives the viewer a full (and believable) tour of the interior human universe, along with the requisite doses of suspense, sex, and sabotage.

FIEND WITHOUT A FACE (1958) B/W. *Dir.:* Arthur Crabtree. *With:* Marshall Thompson, Kim Parker, Terence Kilburn. **74 mins.** Beta, VHS **($39.95).** Blackhawk. ★★

A team of British and American scientists are pursuing a means of translating thought into palpable forms. This is a SF film deserving of its cult status for its excellent horror finale, featuring stop-motion animated brains 'n' spines leaping and latching onto people, sucking their skulls dry, and then getting chopped and shot apart in gory fashion. These effects are amazingly well done (by Austrians Puppel Nordhoff and Peter Nielsen), injecting some exhilarating vigor into the last half of an otherwise pedestrian effort.

FINAL COUNTDOWN, THE (1980) C. *Dir.:* Don Taylor. *With:* Kirk Douglas, James Farentino, Martin Sheen. **104 mins.** Rated PG. Beta, VHS **($79.95);** CED **($29.95).** Vestron. ★½

The British aircraft carrier *Nimitz* collides with an unnatural storm and is sent back in time to "a date which will live in infamy." Captain Douglas deliberates about whether they should interfere with past events and alert ships stationed at Pearl Harbor. In general, a disappointing cruise through waters already patrolled by everything from *The Twilight Zone* to *The Time Tunnel.* A grade-A cast incapacitated by tired TV material.

FINAL PROGRAMME, THE (1973) C. *Dir.:* Robert Fuest. *With:* Jon Finch, Sterling Hayden, Patrick Magee, Jenny Runacre. **87 mins.** Rated R. Beta, VHS **($59.95).** Thorn EMI. ★★★½

A wicked satire of a future ecologic/economic collapse based on the first of Michael Moorcock's "Jerry Cornelius" novels. Finch is delightful as Cornelius, a man of dry wit pursued by a cannibal villainess and a team of scientists who want to reincarnate him as the new Messiah. A British production designed like an incredible comic book, with recognizable character actors present in every scene.

FIRE AND ICE (1983) C. *Dir.:* Ralph Bakshi. *Animated.* **81 mins.** Rated PG. Beta, VHS **($79.95)**; CED **($19.98)**. RCA/Columbia. ★½

Bakshi's long-awaited teaming with fantasy artist *extraordinaire* Frank Frazetta is a disaster—a formulaic sword-and-sorcery saga about a well-muscled hero and a well-bosomed heroine calming the fireworks between two warring factions. Continues Bakshi's recent trend of feature-length rotoscoping (cartoon tracing of live-action footage) and perpetuates his usual racial stereotypes in a fantasy setting. Superficially attractive, but the content is crude, thickheaded, and misogynistic.

Fire and Ice

Firestarter

FIREBIRD 2015 A.D. (1980) C. *Dir.:* David M. Robertson. *With:* Darren McGavin, Doug McClure, George Touliatos. **97 mins.** Rated PG. Beta, VHS **($69.95)**. Embassy. ★½

Would you believe science fiction for good ole boys? In the year 2015, the private automobile is outlawed after a global fuel shortage, resulting in the formation of renegade societies known as "burners"—gun-totin' Southern folk who refuse to turn their guzzlers over to Uncle Sam. Dusty driving sequences prevail here; see *The Last Chase* for a marginally preferable treatment of the theme.

FIRESTARTER (1984) C. *Dir.:* Mark L. Lester. *With:* David Keith, Drew Barrymore, George C. Scott. **115 mins.** Rated R. Beta, VHS **($79.95)**; CED **($29.98)**. MCA. ★½

Barrymore plays Charlie McKee, a girl with the special telekinetic ability to raise the temperature of external objects to the point of inflammation. Features good supporting performances by Martin Sheen, Louise Fletcher, and Moses Gunn, but overall, the movie is shapeless and unfocused. The worst Stephen King film to date.

FIRST SPACESHIP ON VENUS, THE (1964) C. *Dir.:* Kurt Maetzig. *With:* Yoko Tani, Oldrich Lukes, Ignacy Machowski. **78 mins.** No rating. Beta, VHS **($54.95).** VCI. ★★

This German-made adaptation of the early Stanislaw Lem novel *Planet of Death* tells the extremely odd tale of an Earth-to-Venus expedition, circa 1980. The crew is composed of an Oriental woman, a black American, and a German Caucasian male (an unusually fair mix), who discover a Venus dismantled by ages-old nuclear detonations. Quite good, actually, with wholly acceptable alien atmosphere and special effects, but the unusual direction takes some warming up to.

FLASH GORDON (1936). See FLASH GORDON: ROCKETSHIP.

FLASH GORDON (1980) C. *Dir.:* Mike Hodges. *With:* Max Von Sydow, Sam J. Jones, Melody Anderson, Ornella Muti. **111 mins.** Rated PG. Beta, VHS **($39.95);** Laser; CED **($34.98).** MCA. ★★½

Dino De Laurentiis' big-budget filming of Alex Raymond's comic strip has enjoyed a backlash of favor in recent years following its initial bad word of mouth. Actually it's nothing more than an extravagantly polished updating of the old Universal serials with a swaggering Queen score and an unfortunately thick Flash—who, in 45 years, has regressed from a test pilot to a football star! Van Sydow and Ornella Muti couldn't be bettered as Ming and daughter.

FLASH GORDON CONQUERS THE UNIVERSE (1940) B/W. *Dir.:* Ford Beebe and Ray Taylor. *With:* Buster Crabbe, Anne Gwynne, Charles Middleton. **240 mins.** No rating. Beta, VHS **($99.95).** Video Yesteryear. ★★

This entire 12-chapter Universal serial begins with Earth being tormented by a mysterious purple ray from space that is traced by Flash and Dr. Zarkoff back to mysterious planet Mongo. The third and final Flash Gordon serial is the least interesting of the bunch, introducing a new (and less effective) actress as Dale Arden, and inserting misplaced historical elements in its exhausted SF milieu.

FLASH GORDON: MARS ATTACKS THE WORLD (1938) B/W. *Dir.:* Ford Beebe and Robert F. Hill. *With:* Buster Crabbe, Frank Shannon, Charles Middleton. **87 mins.** No rating. Beta, VHS **($N/A).** Video Communications. ★★½

Flash, Dale, and Zarkoff head for Mars to stop thefts of Earth nitrogen and get involved in pacifying warring tribes of tree and clay people. This feature-length condensation of Universal's 15-part serial *Flash Gordon's Trip to Mars* is a slight but noticeable corruption of its predecessor, with some deliberate comedy diluting its natural charm.

FLASH GORDON: ROCKETSHIP (1936) B/W. *Dir.:* Frederick Stephani. *With:* Buster Crabbe, Frank Shannon, Charles Middleton. **75 mins.** No rating. Beta, VHS **($49.95).** Video Yesteryear. ★★★

The condensation of this original *Flash Gordon* serial is recommended for newcomers, but old hands will want to hold out for rare screenings of the full-length version. In many ways, it's the definitive movie serial, featuring charismatic heroes and villains, frightening henchmen, and the cheesiest special effects this side of Mongo. This shorter edition is good, but a comparatively sorry second best. (aka FLASH GORDON.)

FLESH GORDON (1974) C. *Dir.:* Michael Benveneste and Howard Ziehm. *With:* Jason Williams, Suzanne Fields, John Hoyt. **70 mins.** Rated R. Beta, VHS **($54.95).** Media. ★★½

Space hero Flesh Gordon travels into space (in a rudely shaped rocket) with comrades Dale Ardor and Dr. Flexi Jerkoff, where they are imperiled by Emperor Wang, the god Pan, and the dreaded penisaurus. "Not to be confused with the original *Flash Gordon*," indeed! This sometimes *very* funny film was originally a hard-core romp, but the unexpectedly high quality of the film's special effects (by Jim Danforth, David Allen, and Greg Jein) led to a soft-core cutting and mainstream release.

FLIGHT TO MARS (1951) C. *Dir.:* Lesley Selander. *With:* Cameron Mitchell, Marguerite Chapman, Arthur Franz. **72 mins.** No rating. Beta, VHS **($29.95).** Nostalgia Merchant. ★★

A rather uninspired space opera about our first Mars landing, which results in the discovery of a magnificent underground city plotting to invade Earth. Astronaut Franz falls in love with the

Martian leader's daughter, who feels that Earth has a right to live in peace. He takes her aboard his rocket as a willing hostage. One of the last productions of Monogram Studios.

FORBIDDEN PLANET (1956) C. *Dir.:* Fred McLeod Wilcox. *With:* Walter Pidgeon, Leslie Nielsen, Anne Francis. **98 mins.** No rating. Beta, VHS **($59.95)**; Laser **($25.95)**; CED **($19.95)**. MGM/UA. ★★★½

A search party is sent from Earth in the year 2257 to visit the expatriate scientist Morbius on the distant star Altair IV, where he has boosted his IQ to supergenius extremes with the machinery of the extinct Krell civilization. The perfect example of 1950s SF romanticism has low comedy and juvenile sex teasing, not to mention Robby the Robot, and also a startling overall intelligence (the story was lifted from Shakespeare's *The Tempest*). The excellent monster effects were created by Disney animators. Although the all-electronic score has its advocates, it somewhat handicaps an otherwise exciting film.

FORBIDDEN WORLD (1982) C. *Dir.:* Alan Holzman. *With:* Jesse Vint, Dawn Dunlap, Linden Chiles. **82 mins.** Rated R. Beta, VHS **($69.95)**. Embassy. ★½

One of New World Pictures' *Alien* rip-offs produced just before Roger Corman jumped ship, this film features a spaceship under internal attack by a lab-grown mutant with an ever-changing appearance. Dark lighting and a constant avalanche of sweat, blood, and slime make this low-rent production uncomfortably thick-looking, but it moves along briskly under the hand of former editor Holzman. The actresses undress whenever they can. (aka MUTANT.)

FORBIDDEN ZONE (1980) B/W. *Dir.:* Richard Elfman. *With:* Susan Tyrell, Herve Villechaize, Viva. **75 mins.** Rated R. Beta, VHS **($39.95)**. Media. ★★½

This weird, offbeat, one-of-a-kind fantasy takes place in the subterranean "Sixth Dimension," where a horny midget king (guess who?) oversees dancing frogs, the robotized Kipper Kids, bikinied bimboes, and other miscellaneous madness. Events get pretty graphic and appear to have been arbitrarily written around the perky punk score of Oingo Boingo and the delectably bizarre set design. Snub this if you find vomit in movies distasteful.

FORCE BEYOND, THE (1977) C. *Dir.:* William Sachs. *With:* Don Elkins, Peter Byrne, Renee Dahinden. **85 mins.** Rated G. Beta, VHS **($54.95).** Media. ★★

Children aren't believed when they claim to have seen the landing of a flying saucer, and adults pay the consequences. Fairly typical SF fare, inspired by *Invaders From Mars,* from the director of *Galaxina* (see review) and *The Incredible Melting Man.*

FROM THE EARTH TO THE MOON (1958) C. *Dir.:* Byron Haskin. *With:* Joseph Cotten, George Sanders, Debra Paget. **100 mins.** No rating. Beta, VHS **($54.95).** VCI. ★★

So-so Jules Verne adaptation about a Civil War-era scientist catapulting the first manned rocket to the moon. Fine effects and competent direction aren't enough to overcome the dreadful sentimentality of the script, which plays down the wonder of defiling the moon's virginity in favor of a dull, budding romance between Cotten and Paget.

FURY, THE (1979) C. *Dir.:* Brian De Palma. *With:* Kirk Douglas, Amy Irving, John Cassavetes. **118 mins.** Rated R. Beta, VHS **($59.98).** CBS/Fox. ★★½

Two telekinetic teens, their powers misdirected by the government against its enemies, escape and lash out against organizations that would reharness them. The film makes an interesting point about the impossibility of restoring an innocence that has been perverted. Otherwise a typical De Palma film— gorgeous but full of blood and pyrotechnic imagery.

FUTUREWORLD (1976) C. *Dir.:* Richard T. Heffron. *With:* Peter Fonda, Blythe Danner, Arthur Hill. **107 mins.** Rated PG. Beta, VHS **($39.98);** CED **($29.95).** Warner. ★★★

This *Westworld* sequel is fairly entertaining. Two journalists covering the grand opening of the robotized amusement park of *Westworld* fame uncover a plan to substitute mechanized doubles for politicians. The tired aspects of the plot are somewhat revitalized by the amusingly naive chemistry between the two leads (Fonda calls Danner "Socks"), and a nice cameo by Stuart Margolin.

GALAXINA (1980) C. *Dir.:* William Sachs. *With:* Dorothy Stratten, Avery Schreiber, James David Hinton. **95 mins.** Rated R. Beta, VHS **($59.95);** Laser **($29.98).** MCA. ★½

The slovenly space crusader Captain Butt must retrieve the Blue Star, a powerful gem, from the biomechanical bad guy Ondric. This no-budget SF parody covers only familiar ground, but has retained a foothold in public consciousness as one of late Playmate Stratten's few movie vehicles. As a formidably cool robot who becomes academically interested in emotions, finally learning to enjoy them herself, she displays a germ of talent all the more touching for having never grown.

Galaxina

Galaxy Invader

GALAXY INVADER (1985) C. *Dir.:* Don Dohler. *With:* Richard Ruxton, Faye Tilles, George Stover. **90 mins.** Rated PG. Beta, VHS **($59.95).** VCI. ★

The packaging for this backyard-born production says, "It came from a galaxy far, far away, an alien explorer—it's mission . . . TO KILL." It's mission turns out to be saving its own scaly, rubber, alien butt from a bunch of redneck sportsmen who fancy its head mounted in somebody's den. Dohler's latest shows some slight improvement over earlier epics like *The Alien Factor* (see review), but it's still not worth the viewer's time.

GALAXY OF TERROR (1981) C. *Dir.:* B.D. Clark. *With:* Erin Moran, Edward Albert, Ray Walston, Sid Haig. **85 mins.** Rated R. Beta, VHS **($69.95).** Embassy. ★★

A group of earnest space travelers investigate an unknown planet, learning that it has the facility to manifest their deepest fears. A high-camp cast, clever explication, and an outrageous rape by a space maggot (worthy of John Waters!) boost this *Alien* imitation into the "must see" class for a certain type of viewer. Those with sharp eyes will note the McDonald's trays lining the walls of the spacecraft.

GHIDRAH THE THREE-HEADED MONSTER (1965) C. *Dir.:* Inoshiro Honda. *With:* Yuriko Hoshi, Yosuke Natsuki, Emi and Yumi
Itoh. **85 mins.** No rating. Beta, VHS **($19.95).** Prism ★★½

Excellent Eiji Tsuburaya special effects distinguish this first
Japanese monster tripleheader (pun intended) which joins Godzilla, Mothra, and Rodan in the common cause of protecting Earth
against a flying, three-headed dragon from space. This film literally has everything, from romance to action to espionage to comedy. Fun to watch, but sad in hindsight as it presages series'
downfall into witless juvenalia.

GLADIATORS, THE (1969) C. *Dir.:* Peter Watkins. *With:* Arthur
Pentelow, Frederick Danner, Kenneth Lo. **105 mins.** No rating.
Beta, VHS **($49.95).** Wizard. ★★½

Watkin's intriguing follow-up to *The War Game* (see review)
looks ahead to a future where all political conflicts are resolved by
a military Olympiad. When the controlling computer systems
suffer a malfunction, man must learn to bridge the distance he's
placed between himself and other men. The premise is ambitious
and intelligent, but production limitations and Watkin's documen-
tarian bent result in an unfortunately pallid movie. (aka THE
PEACE GAME.)

GLEN OR GLENDA? (1953) B/W. *Dir.:* Edward D. Wood, Jr. *With:*
Daniel Davis, Bela Lugosi, Dolores Fuller, Lyle Talbot. **61 mins.**
No rating. Beta, VHS **($39.95).** Video Yesteryear. ★★

Wood's "adults only" transvestism fantasy is among his best-
loved films, and undoubtedly his most perverse, original, and
personal. Wood himself (using the name Daniel Davis) plays a
man driven by the fantasy of wearing his girlfriend's angora
sweater while being simultaneously haunted by infernal demons,
conscience-symbol Lugosi (whose narration must be the most
hilariously opaque in the history of the medium), and visions of
paranoia. In a memorable gaffe, Paramount rereleased the film in
1981 with a serious, full-page ad in *The New York Times!*

GODZILLA: KING OF THE MONSTERS (1956) B/W. *Dir.:* Inoshiro
Honda and Terry Morse. *With:* Raymond Burr, Takashi Shimura,
Akira Takarada. **98 mins.** No rating. Beta, VHS **($59.95);** Laser
($34.95); CED **($29.95).** Vestron. ★★★

Though its many sequels run the gamut from naive to just
plain ridiculous, this first film in the interminable series is con-

foundingly good, with a fascinating pessimistic tint and relentless atmosphere of apocalypse. Raymond Burr (in scenes especially filmed for the American market) comments on the discovery of the radioactive saurian and his climactic assault on Tokyo. The symbolic relationship with Hiroshima and Nagasaki is very much up front.

GODZILLA VS. MONSTER ZERO (1970) C. *Dir.:* Inoshiro Honda. *With:* Nick Adams, Akira Takarada, Jun Tazaki. **93 mins.** Rated G. Beta, VHS **($37.95).** Paramount. ★½
Godzilla and Rodan are placed in hibernation bubbles and sent to Planet X, where Ghidrah the three-headed monster is giving Oriental aliens a lousy time. Earth's good will is repaid when Planet X sends back all three monsters to wipe out mankind! Made in 1966 and released to theaters as *Monster X,* it's a turkey with some joke value. (aka MONSTER X.)

GODZILLA VS. MOTHRA (1963) C. *Dir.:* Inoshiro Honda. *With:* Akira Takarada, Yuriko Hoshi, Emi and Yumi Itoh. **90 mins.** No rating. Beta, VHS **($37.95).** Paramount. ★★½
Pretty much the last gasp of quality as far as the Godzilla films go. The giant moth Mothra battles Godzilla, loses, but has the last laugh by leaving behind a giant egg that hatches gigantic twin cocoon-spitting caterpillars. Sounds awful, but the film (shown in theaters as *Godzilla Vs. The Thing*) features superb color, dazzling effects, and lots of action.

GOLDEN VOYAGE OF SINBAD, THE (1973) C. *Dir.:* Gordon Hessler. *With:* John Phillip Law, Caroline Munro, Tom Baker. **104 mins.** Rated G. Beta, VHS **($69.95).** RCA/Columbia. ⌑® ★★★
Sinbad sets sail for the fabled isle of Lemuria, where he hopes to find the missing piece of a three-jewelled amulet. Ray Harryhausen's second Sinbad opus (following *The 7th Voyage of Sinbad,* see review) is very well done, with several marvelous stop-motion animation sequences which pit the sailor against the deadly supernatural pawns of the Black Prince Khoura. But the film doesn't amaze as often as it should. Exotic atmosphere is helped immeasurably by Miklos Rosza's score.

GOLEM, THE (1920) B/W. *Dir.:* Paul Wegener. *With:* Paul Wegener, Albert Steinruck, Ernst Deutsch. **94 mins.** Beta, VHS **($49.95).** Video Yesteryear. ★★★★

A silent classic about a life-size clay man who, upon being awakened by the intonation of a secret Hebrew word, protects persecuted Jews. As with the earlier 1914 version, director Wegener himself plays the clay man with an air of indomitable heaviness, stomping through the hauntingly medieval streets of Prague and facing blind opposition. A must-see, one of several fantasy classics photographed by the great Karl Freund. The film had an inestimable impact on James Whale's *Frankenstein* of 1931.

GORATH (1962) C. *Dir.:* Inoshiro Honda. *With:* Ryo Ikebe, Jun Tazaki, Akihiko Hirata. **77 mins.** Rated G. Beta, VHS **($N/A).** Video Gems. ★★
A collision between Earth and the approaching planet Gorath is avoided by shifting our orbit with a surge of rocket fire. It saves our necks, but also awakens a giant prehistoric walrus frozen beneath the Arctic waters. A little seen monster extravaganza from Tokyo's *Godzillameister* Honda, even less of which was seen when the American distributor removed the monster scenes for the sake of a more serious, scientific production. Intact, it's said to be one of Honda's better pictures.

GORGO (1961) C. *Dir.:* Eugène Lourié. *With:* Bill Travers, William Sylvester, Vincent Winter. **78 mins.** No rating. Beta, VHS **($39.95).** Video Dimensions. ★★★
A giant sea monster surfaces off the Scottish coastline and gets lassoed and sold to the circus circuit by two opportunistic fishermen, who learn too late that it is only an *infant* specimen and that Mama's in hot pursuit. This British production is highly recommended, featuring excellent special effects (including the best man-in-a-suit monster *ever*) and a narrative warmth that makes it ideal for older children. Lourié's directorial career consisted of three movies, all about sea monsters (*The Beast From 20,000 Fathoms* and *The Giant Behemoth* remain unavailable on video).

GREASER'S PALACE (1972) C. *Dir.:* Robert Downey. *With:* Albert Henderson, Allan Arbus, Michael Sullivan. **91 mins.** No rating. Beta, VHS **($59.95).** RCA/Columbia. ★★★
A surreal tale of an Old West drifter (Arbus) gifted with Christ-like abilities for healing, water-walking, and resurrection, who attempts the unlikely redemption of a sadistic owner of title sa-

loon. This stylish, outrageous fantasy has enough *outre* elements to satisfy the most demanding appetites for the bizarre, with Seaweedhead Greaser's sad family life a clear anticipation of folks later invented by John Waters. Outspoken and great fun, but obviously not for everyone.

GULLIVER'S TRAVELS (1939) C. *Dir.:* Dave Fleischer. *Animated.* **74 mins.** No rating. Beta, VHS **($19.95)**; Laser **($34.95)**; CED **($29.95)**. Crown, Kartes, World. Vestron (disc only). ★★½

Fleischer Studio's first animated feature is a disappointment on both animated and literary counts, mixing stilted rotoscoping techniques with full cartoon animation, and hideously trivializing Swift's satiric masterpiece. The film only covers Gulliver's visit to Lilliput, where he settles a petty argument between two kingdoms, making marriage possible for their respective prince and princess. The running time is filled out by mediocre musical numbers.

HANGAR 18 (1980) C. *Dir.:* James L. Conway. *With:* Darren McGavin, Robert Vaughn, Gary Collins. **97 mins.** Rated PG. Beta, VHS **($49.95)**. Worldvision. ★½

A dismal "speculation" drama about aliens being held hostage for experimentation and testing by an arm of the U.S. Government. The special effects are just barely competent, which is all that can be said for the overall production. *Wavelength* (see review) offers a far more intriguing treatment of the same theme.

HEARTBEEPS (1981) C. *Dir.:* Allan Arkush. *With:* Andy Kaufman, Bernadette Peters, Randy Quaid. **79 mins.** Rated PG. Beta, VHS **($39.95)**. MCA. ★★★

A charming SF-comedy about two personable robots who fall in love and escape from a factory to pursue their own lives. Late comedian Kaufman's only feature, it was misunderstood by Universal and badly butchered (note the short running time) prior to release, but is still warmly recommended. Stan Winston's superlative Oscar-nominated, robot makeup results in numerable, marvelous supporting "characters."

HEAVY TRAFFIC (1973) C. *Dir.:* Ralph Bakshi. *Animated.* **76 mins.** Rated X. Beta, VHS **($59.95)**. Warner. ★★★

An underground comic-book artist escapes from his urban nightmare by delving into his work, parodying his despair in pencil and ink. Bakshi's intense, personal follow-up to *Fritz the Cat* takes his unique animation into brave new worlds, introducing live-action backgrounds, hard violence, and bizarre characters plucked from NYC's underbelly. It's too extreme for some viewers, but the film's unflinching honesty makes this Bakshi's best work.

HERCULES (1959) C. *Dir.:* Pietro Francisci. *With:* Steve Reeves, Sylva Koscina, Ivo Garrani. **107 mins.** No rating. Beta, VHS **($59.95).** Embassy. ★★★

Although it encompasses only two of the mythic strongman's twelve labors, this Italian-made extravaganza was undeserving of the condescending criticism it received in its day. Today it looks quite spectacular, photographed with colorful and expressionistic lighting by Mario Bava. Reeves' charisma is still unequalled in films of this type. It led to innumerable sequels, none of which have yet been released on video.

Hercules (1983)   Ice Pirates

HERCULES (1983) C. *Dir.:* Lewis Coates (Luigi Cozzi). *With:* Lou Ferrigno, Sybil Danning, Brad Harris. **100 mins.** Rated PG. Beta, VHS **($79.95);** Laser **($34.95).** MGM/UA. ☐® ★

This is not a remake of the Reeves semi-classic, but rather a preposterous, money-grubbing movie that fills the screen with every commercial SF element from large breasts to laser blasts. Ferrigno is a very dull lead, battling robot bugs sent his way by villianess Danning. Supporting player Harris played Hercules himself in several 1960s productions.

HOBBIT, THE (1977) C. *Dir.:* Arthur Rankin, Jr. and Jules Bass. *Animated.* **78 mins.** No rating. Beta, VHS **($34.95).** Sony. ★★★

Hobbit Bilbo Baggins teams with a troupe of dwarves to retrieve a stolen treasure from Smaug, the fire-breathing dragon. In spite of its limitations, this musical made-for-TV cartoon of J.R.R. Tolkien's introduction to his *Lord of the Rings* trilogy surpasses Ralph Bakshi's. The voices are supplied by Orson Bean (as Bilbo Baggins), John Huston, and the great Brother Theodore.

HORROR PLANET (1982) C. *Dir.:* Norman J. Warren. *With:* Judy Geeson, Robin Clarke, Stephanie Beacham. **93 mins.** Rated R. Beta, VHS **($69.95).** Embassy. ★★
The crew of a spaceship is placed in the absurd position of defending itself against an expectant mother (Geeson) who's been impregnated by an alien horror. Occasionally interesting and unceasingly grim, the film has a hard-working cast and a relentless screenplay but is hurt by confusing photography and bland editing. Geeson, conveying an alien evil through facial expressions alone, is especially chilling.

HUMAN EXPERIMENTS, THE (1980) C. *Dir.:* Gregory Goodell. *With:* Linda Haynes, Aldo Ray, Jackie Coogan, Ellen Travolta. **82 mins.** Rated R. Beta, VHS **($39.95).** VidAmerica. ★½
A female singer without family or friends is falsely accused of murder and imprisoned in a women's correctional facility where a psychiatrist is conducting vague mind control experiments. Baffling and senseless, this is not much in the way of SF, even though VidAmerica is selling it that way.

I MARRIED A MONSTER FROM OUTER SPACE (1958) B/W. *Dir.:* Gene Fowler, Jr. *With:* Tom Tryon, Gloria Talbott. **78 mins.** No Rating. Beta, VHS **($44.95).** Paramount. ★★★
Newlywed Tryon has his body overtaken by the soul of a putty-faced alien, with his wife Talbott gradually sensing the estrangement. Among the best of the lesser known SF films of the '50s, with smart direction and eerie special effects. Makes a neat double bill with the original *Invasion of The Body Snatchers*.

ICE PIRATES (1984) C. *Dir.:* Stuart Raffill. *With:* Robert Urich, Mary Crosby, Michael D. Roberts. **93 mins.** Rated PG. Beta, VHS **($79.95);** Laser **($34.95).** MGM/UA. ★½
The title refers to the occupation of the film's heroes, who raid ice tankers in a nebulous future when water is a precious commodity. This overdone, pseudocomedy rips off every element from every popular SF film of recent years (cute robots, bitchy

Princess, etc.), tossing in some rating-straining extras like a razor-toothed castration machine. Scores half an inch above rock bottom, thanks to an honest, embarrassed-looking cast.

IMPULSE (1984) C. *Dir.:* Graham Baker. *With:* Meg Tilly, Tim Matheson, Hume Cronyn. **95 mins.** Rated R. Beta, VHS **($79.95);** Laser **($29.98);** CED. Vestron. ★★

A chemical contaminating the milk sold in the small town of Sutcliffe, U.S.A., totally erases the behavioral inhibitions of its villagers, as well as the distinction between *thinking* something and *doing* something. A reverse-image companion piece to *The Invasion of the Body Snatchers* that wanders astray with unsympathetically vacant performances and misguided tensions.

INCREDIBLE HULK, THE (1977) C. *Dir.:* Kenneth Johnson. *With:* Bill Bixby, Lou Ferrigno, Susan Sullivan. **100 mins.** No rating. Beta, VHS **($39.95).** MCA. ★★

This CBS-TV pilot, which led to a successful series, dramatizes the origin of the title character, a muscular green alter ego that developed in scientist Bixby after a bombardment of gamma rays. The film takes considerable license with the Marvel Comics character, replacing camp elements with surprising, bittersweet sentimentality, but it made a solid foundation for the show. Sullivan stands out as Bixby's love-smitten assistant.

INCREDIBLE SHRINKING WOMAN, THE (1981) C. *Dir.:* Joel Schumacher. *With:* Lily Tomlin, Charles Grodin, Henry Gibson. **88 mins.** Rated PG. Beta, VHS **($39.95);** Laser **($29.98).** MCA. ★★½

A combination of chemicals in commonplace consumer goods reduces housewife Tomlin to matchstick size, and elevates her to such a celebrity status that she becomes a product herself. Shares only the premise with the Jack Arnold/Richard Matheson classic *The Incredible Shrinking Man,* using it as a launching pad for an attack against the thoughtlessness of the advertising world. Good effects, with a super cameo by Rick Baker as a charming gorilla, but a prevalent air of bias overwhelms the imagination of the piece.

INFRA-MAN (1976) C. *Dir.:* Hua-Shan. *With:* Li Hsiu-Hsien, Wang Hsieh, Terry Liu. **92 mins.** Rated R. Beta, VHS **($49.95).** Prism. ★★★

A scientist creates the bionic superhero Infra-Man just in time to deflect an attack by the infamous Princess Dragon Mom and her hoard of tentacled monsters. One of the rare Japanese exploitation films in recent years to achieve amiability by overcramming itself with colorful foolishness. It's funny how, just moments after being created and christened, Infra-Man's first public appearance is heralded by cries of, "Look! It's Infra-Man!"

INVADERS FROM MARS (1953) C. *Dir.:* William Cameron Menzies. *With:* Arthur Franz, Helena Carter, Jimmy Hunt. **78 mins.** No rating. Beta, VHS **($49.95).** Nostalgia Merchant. ★★★

If you've been a science fiction fan since childhood, you probably love the memory of this haunting tale of extraterrestrial paranoia. A little boy sees a flying saucer land on the hill outside his bedroom window, but no one will believe him becaue he's an imaginative little boy (and because most of the authority figures in his life suddenly develop little switches on the backs of their necks!). Seen afresh, it's far from perfect, but to a large extent, it recaptures that mythic time when a boy's best friends were his pretty schoolteacher and the town's scientist.

INVASION OF THE BEE GIRLS, THE (1973) C. *Dir.:* Denis Sanders. *With:* William Smith, Anitra Ford, Victoria Vetri. **85 mins.** Rated R. Beta, VHS **($59.95).** Embassy. ★★★

This SF exploitation film scripted by Nicholas Meyer is amusing, titillating (hence classic) drive-in fare. Smith comes to a small town to investigate a sequence of deaths attributed to sexual exhaustion but actually caused by area housewives who metamorphose into half-bee, half-women beings. Shot in fluorescent colors at stilted angles, the film unreels like an irresistibly raunchy comic book.

INVASION OF THE BODY SNATCHERS (1956) C. *Dir.:* Don Siegel. *With:* Kevin McCarthy, Dana Wynter, Carolyn Jones. **80 mins.** No rating. Beta, VHS **($59.95);** CED **($19.98).** Republic. ★★★★

A family doctor returns to his hometown to discover his patients are being possessed by aliens. The film documents the struggle of the doctor and his loved ones to stay awake (the only way of remaining unpossessed) and to alert the authorities. A classic of the genre, briskly and tersely directed by action-great Siegel, that also makes subtle editorial comments about the political climate of its time.

INVASION OF THE BODY SNATCHERS (1978) C. *Dir.:* Philip Kaufman. *With:* Donald Sutherland, Veronica Cartwright, Jeff Goldblum. **115 mins.** Rated PG. Beta Hi-Fi, VHS **($59.95);** Laser **($34.95);** CED **($19.98).** MGM/UA. ★★★★

A remake worthy of viewing in tandem with its original. Sutherland is cast as a San Francisco health official investigating the dehumanizing effects of flower buds on various personalities. The film unveils many clever and shocking set-pieces; the collection of disorienting sounds and images emphasizes how peculiar our world might look to an alien intelligence.

INVASION OF THE BODY STEALERS (1969) C. *Dir.:* Gerry Levy. *With:* George Sanders, Maurice Evans, Neil Connery. **91 mins.** Rated PG. Beta, VHS **($49.95).** USA. ★½

A British-made SF film about the momentary disappearance of paratroopers in mid-fall, when their bodies are abducted and replaced by alien surrogates. The interesting cast is unable to rescue this flimsy, unoriginal invasion picture. Visually flat and directed without personality or enthusiasm.

ISLAND AT THE TOP OF THE WORLD, THE (1974) C. *Dir.:* Robert Stevenson. *With:* David Hartman, Donald Sinden, Mako. **89 mins.** Rated G. Beta, VHS **($69.95).** Disney. ★★

An airship search (in 1908, no less) for a missing adventurer leads an expedition into uncharted arctic regions where an island populated by a primitive Viking people is discovered. One of the Disney Studios less-inspired Jules Verne-style adaptations, this film is more tiresome for adult viewers than it ought to be, with disappointing special effects by the usually reliable Harrison and Peter Ellenshaw.

ISLAND OF DR. MOREAU, THE (1977) C. *Dir.:* Don Taylor. *With:* Burt Lancaster, Michael York, Barbara Carrera. **98 mins.** Rated PG. Beta, VHS **($59.95);** CED **($29.95).** Warner. ★★★

This remake of the classic *Island of Lost Souls* outlines the experiments of the island patriarch Lancaster, who is returning human beings to their animalistic origins in his "house of pain." Unlike the original, which was draped in darkness and mystery, this version is bright and colorful, relying on the performances for its anxious atmosphere. Thanks to York, who brilliantly conveys the physical confusion and agony of de-evolution, the picture comes surprisingly close to its mark.

IT CAME FROM OUTER SPACE (1953) B/W. *Dir.:* Jack Arnold. *With:* Richard Carlson, Barbara Rush, Russell Johnson. **81 mins.** No rating. Bcta, VHS **($62.95)**. VMC. ★★½

A glowing meteor containing an alien presence crashes into the desert. Its arrival is observed only by astronomer Carlson, who must contend with numerous alien duplications of neighboring townsfolk in his struggle to be believed. Heavy on atmosphere and eerie visuals, this was among the first 3-D releases and the first of several increasingly brilliant SF films from director Arnold (whose masterpiece, *The Incredible Shrinking Man,* remains unavailable to video).

JABBERWOCKY (1977) C. *Dir.:* Terry Gilliam. *With:* Michael Palin, Max Wall, Deborah Fallender. **104 mins.** Rated PG. Beta, VHS **($59.95)**; Laser **($29.95)**. RCA/Columbia. ★★½

Popularly known as a Monty Python comedy, this medieval slice of fantasy features only one member of the Python troupe (Palin) and plays better as a jolly fantasy than as a grim comedy. An innocent boy arrives in a kingdom, only to find its people resigned to sacrificing their daughters to "the manxome foe" so they can live in peace. The superb medieval atmosphere and Jabberwock (designed by Valerie Charlton and Clinton Cavers, following Tenniel's blueprint) make this uneven film worth sitting through.

It Came From Outer Space

Jason and the Argonauts

JASON AND THE ARGONAUTS (1963) C. *Dir.:* Don Chaffey. *With:* Todd Armstrong, Nancy Kovack, Gary Raymond. **104 mins.** No rating. Beta, VHS **($59.95)**; Laser **($29.95)**; CED **($19.98)**. RCA/Columbia. ★★★★

Arguably the best of several films distinguished by the stop-motion animation of Ray Harryhausen, this movie chronicles the legend of Jason's search for the Golden Fleece. Its imaginative perspective has Zeus controlling our hero's actions from Mount Olympus with chessboard pieces of him and his fellow adventurers. The mortals confront and overcome such dazzling obstacles as gigantic iron statues, sword-wielding skeletons, harpies, and the many-headed Hydra. This mythologically sound scenario is terrific entertainment.

JULES VERNE'S FANTASTIC BALLOON VOYAGE (1982) C. *With:* Hugo Stiglitz, Jeff Cooper, Carl East. **100 mins.** Rated G. Beta, VHS **($39.95).** Video Gems. ★★

An Italian "remake" of *Around the World in 80 Days* made on a budget that would scarcely pay for such a trip in real life. (aka THE FANTASTIC BALLOON VOYAGE.)

KEEP, THE (1983) C. *Dir.:* Michael Mann. *With:* Scott Glenn, Ian McKellen, Alberta Watson. **96 mins.** Rated R. Beta, VHS **($59.95);** Laser **($29.95).** Paramount. ★½

In WWII Rumania, the Nazis discover an ancient, immense fortress studded with nickel crucifixes that holds a mysterious force of ambiguous will. After it has been partially freed, a silver-eyed stranger (Glenn) appears to fulfill his destiny. This incoherent fantasy with horrific overtones is burdened by numb, superficial direction, ill-fitting gloss, and a slow pace.

KING KONG (1933) B/W. *Dir.:* Ernest B. Schoedsack and Merian C. Cooper. *With:* Robert Armstrong, Fay Wray, Bruce Cabot. **105 mins.** No rating. Beta, VHS **($49.95);** Laser; CED **($19.98).** Nostalgia Merchant. Criterion (laser only). ★★★★

Adventurer/showman Armstrong saves Wray from a Depression-era breadline and takes her on an ocean cruise to Skull Island, where he teams her with the tallest, darkest leading man in show business. You can't be a movie lover unless you've seen this fantasy classic at least twice; the breathtaking finale atop the newly completed Empire State Building is a cornerstone event in the history of the medium. Willis O'Brien's stop-motion animation is only ever so slightly crude in light of modern accomplishments, but his work here is all the more charming for it and will live forever. The laserdisc version includes a running commentary by film historian Ronald Haver.

KING KONG (1976) C. *Dir.:* John Guillermin. *With:* Jeff Bridges, Jessica Lange, Charles Grodin. **135 mins.** Rated PG. Beta, VHS **($66.95);** Laser **($35.95);** CED **($29.98),** Paramount. ★★
The only reasons for remaking the quintessential Hollywood classic were commercial, but gross incompetence is the only excuse for this colossal, celluloid turkey. Producer De Laurentiis invested millions in a 40-foot Kong robot that never worked, so makeup wizard Rick Baker was recruited to play the part (without screen credit) in a superbly articulated ape suit. (Carlo Rambaldi, who built the *robot,* copped the Special Effects Oscar!) Lorenzo Semple's script is laboriously pun heavy, and it's a tribute to Lange's talent and resilience that she was able to overcome our memory of it.

KING OF KONG ISLAND (1978) C. *Dir.:* Robert Morris. *With:* Brad Harris, Marc Lawrence, Esmeralda Barros. **92 mins.** Rated R. Beta, VHS **($44.95).** VCI. ★
Former Hercules Harris is sent to Kong Island to deal with a mad doctor busy automating the brains of the isle's simian inhabitants. Despite the title, there is nothing remotely similar to *King Kong* in this stupid SF-action vehicle, which appears to have been produced as a showcase for the topless Barros. Made in Spain.

KING OF THE ROCKET MEN (1949) B/W. *Dir.:* Fred Brannon. *With:* Tristam Coffin, Mae Clarke, House Peters, Jr. **280 mins.** No rating. Beta, VHS **($79.95).** Republic. ★★★
Coffin is A-OK as Dr. King, a cracker jack scientist who invents a rocket suit which he then dons to battle the diabolical Dr. Vulcan. This is gloriously naive fun, full of action and humor (the dial on King's jetpack reads "Up, Down, Fast, Slow"!) but *long,* and therefore best swallowed in short doses. The 12-part Republic serial is one of the best of its kind.

KRONOS (1957) B/W. *Dir.:* Kurt Neumann. *With:* Jeff Morrow, Barbara Lawrence, John Emery. **78 mins.** No rating. Beta, VHS **($49.95).** Nostalgia Merchant. ★★½
This minor SF classic from the fifties sports one of the era's few unique angles: The space visitors don't invade Earth, but instead drop off a gigantic machine which proceeds to walk across the continents, crushing cities and people with its pummelling footfalls. Morrow and Lawrence play scientists looking for a way to save the planet from destruction. The special effects,

combined with life-size props and excellent animation, are never less than interesting.

KRULL (1983) C. *Dir.:* Peter Yates. *With:* Ken Marshall, Lysette Anthony, Freddie Jones. **117 mins.** Rated PG. Beta Hi-Fi, VHS **($79.95);** Laser **($34.95);** CED **($19.95).** RCA/Columbia. ★★
  This well-mounted but uninvolving fantasy opens as the marriage of the hero and the princess is disrupted when she is abducted by invading hordes from an ominous, flying mountain. The hero, who sets off to obtain a special amulet needed to free her, is befriended by a collection of odd but lovable characters and encounters strange and miraculous sights. It's another load of mythology and weird names to memorize, but *why bother?* Anthony's performance was doctored in post-production with an American actress redubbing all her lines; Yates fared far better with his next production, *The Dresser.*

LAND THAT TIME FORGOT, THE (1975) C. *Dir.:* Kevin Connor. *With:* Doug McClure, Susan Penhaligon, Anthony Ainley. **90 mins.** Rated PG. Beta, VHS **($59.95).** Vestron. ★½
  The first of Amicus Productions' three Edgar Rice Burroughs adaptations, scripted by SF giant Michael Moorcock, is a misproduced tale of a WWI submarine that discovers an area of South America untouched by time and filled with Neanderthals, dinosaurs, and volcanoes. Paunchy McClure is out of his league in the heroic lead against equally unsuitable rubber saurians. The film's sequels, *People That Time Forgot* and *At the Earth's Core,* are also available on video; don't ask us why.

LASERBLAST (1978) C. *Dir.:* Michael Raye. *With:* Kim Milford, Keenan Wynn, Roddy McDowall. **85 mins.** Rated PG. Beta, VHS **($29.95).** Media. ★★
  Two aliens eliminate an extraterrestrial enemy but neglect to take its laser pistol with them. The weapon is later discovered by a teen with a chip on his shoulder. Using the pistol against his enemies, he gradually transmutes into a member of the species responsible for its design. Amateurish but watchable; at its best when David Allen's stop-motion aliens are on screen.

LAST CHASE, THE (1980) C. *Dir.:* Martyn Burke. *With:* Lee Majors, Chris Makepeace, Burgess Meredith. **106 mins.** Rated PG. Beta, VHS **($79.95);** CED **($29.95).** Vestron. ★★

When the Earth's oil supplies have been depleted, all governments circulate anti-machine propoganda and declare all transportation vehicles illegal. Lee Majors rebels against this posttechnological future by stealing the last automobile and heading West, where the effects of a devastating plague remain unknown. This bland SF film has an occasional interesting special effect, otherwise it goes nowhere fast.

LAST DAYS OF MAN ON EARTH, THE (1973) C. *Dir.:* Robert Fuest. *With:* Jon Finch, Sterling Hayden, Patrick Magee, Jenny Runacre. **70 mins.** Rated R. Beta, VHS **($69.95).** Embassy. ★★½

A shortened version of *The Final Programme* (see review) prepared by Roger Corman for its American release. Less bitter than the original, but also with less biting satire: Some of Sterling Hayden's best moments were left on the cutting room floor. The full-length version is actually cheaper!

Krull

The Last Starfighter

LAST STARFIGHTER, THE (1984) C. *Dir.:* Nick Castle. *With:* Lance Guest, Catherine Mary Stewart, Robert Preston. **100 mins.** Rated PG. Beta, VHS **($79.95);** CED **($29.98).** MCA. ★★½

Guest's prowess at video games is monitored by emmissaries from the Star League of Planets, which recruits him to defend their frontiers from evil invaders. It's sporadically entertaining, but full enjoyment is inhibited by the feeble premise and the elementary development of the plot. On the plus side, the special effects (achieved via computer animation—*not* miniatures) are unusual looking and well done.

LIQUID SKY (1983) C. *Dir.:* Slava Tsukerman. *With:* Anne Carlisle, Paula Sheppard, Bob Brady. **112 mins.** Rated R. Beta, VHS **($59.95).** Media. ★★½

Aliens land on a Bowery rooftop, thirsting for a heroin-like substance released in the human bloodstream following orgasm, and use a model to obtain it for them through intercourse. This homemade feature shot in NYC locations won a hard-core cult following with its new-wave trappings, rabidly perverse scenario, and Carlisle's alert-as-a-zombie, bisexual double role. However offbeat, the film is uncomfortably cold, posturing, and overlong.

LOGAN'S RUN (1976) C. *Dir.:* Michael Anderson. *With:* Michael York, Jenny Agutter, Peter Ustinov. **119 mins.** Rated PG. Beta, VHS **($59.95);** Laser **($34.95);** CED **($19.95).** MGM/UA. ★½

It's the year 2274 and people over 30 are turned to sand and swept away by sandmen. One crafty mortal (York) elects to escape his nearing fate as well as the civilization that adopted the practice. This is glossy but inescapably stupid SF, full of unconvincing, costly effects and preachy writing. Ustinov appears in a cameo role as the planet's only free man, and his performance reveals an acute awareness of stand-up comedy for someone who's presumably never seen television.

LOOKER (1981) C. *Dir.:* Michael Crichton. *With:* Albert Finney, James Coburn, Susan Dey. **93 mins.** Rated PG. Beta, VHS **($64.95).** Warner. ★½

Good performances and effects are the only distinguishing qualities in this confused (and confusing) tale in which TV mogul Coburn develops three-dimensional copies of beautiful models after the originals are murdered. Finney is surprisingly good in the thankless role of the plastic surgeon caught up in this mess. Beautiful women and ugly events abound.

LORD OF THE RINGS, THE (1978) C. *Dir.:* Ralph Bakshi. *Animated.* **133 mins.** Rated PG. Beta, VHS **($39.95);** CED **($29.98).** Thorn EMI. ★½

Bakshi's long-awaited filming of J.R.R. Tolkien's trilogy—in which hobbit Frodo Baggins sets out to destroy the Master Ring that threatens to hold his people enslaved—is a visual treat, ripe with rich and colorful animation, but a narrative and structural disaster. Choppy and meandering, the story actually concludes without either a resolution or a warning (Bakshi intends to complete the movie...*someday*), which, in our opinion, makes this a little worse than no movie at all.

LOST PLANET AIRMEN (1949) B/W. *Dir.:* Fred Brannon. *With:* Tristam Coffin, Mae Clarke, House Peters, Jr. **65 mins.** No rating. Beta, VHS **($39.95).** Admit One. ★½

This feature film condensation of the terrific *King of the Rocket Men* serial (see review) is a drastic reduction that lays waste to the naive fun, not to mention *sense,* of the original.

LOST WORLD, THE (1925) B/W. *Dir.:* Harry Hoyt. *With:* Bessie Love, Wallace Beery, Lewis Stone. **60 mins.** No rating. Beta, VHS **($49.95).** Video Yesteryear. ★★★

This silent film of Conan Doyle's story about prehistoric life being discovered on a jungle plateau makes for remarkably good contemporary viewing, thanks to the pioneering stop-motion animation of Willis O'Brien. For the first time, man stared in amazement as dinosaurs lived and breathed (remember, despite what the movies tell you, that our two species never shared the planet together). A tremendous improvement on the more widely seen 1960 remake, it concludes with the flattening of London under the tonnage of a wandering brontosaurus!

MAD MAX (1980) C. *Dir.:* George Miller. *With:* Mel Gibson, Joanne Samuel, Hugh Keays-Byrne. **90 mins.** Rated R. Beta, VHS **($69.95);** Laser **($34.95);** CED **($29.95).** Vestron. ★★★

In the near future, the roads are so overrun by violent gangs that special police units are kept on constant vigil. When the title character's partner is burned alive, he quits the force but finds the problem pursuing him into his private holiday. This brilliant, energetic SF-action piece offers a host of chillingly perverse characters (one credit reads, "And Hugh Keays-Byrne as the Toecutter"!) and an equal number of breathtaking stunts. Its world-acclaimed sequel: *The Road Warrior.*

MADAME SIN (1972) C. *Dir.:* David Greene. *With:* Bette Davis, Rogert Wagner, Denholm Elliott. **73 mins.** No rating. Beta, VHS **($59.98).** CBS/Fox. ★★½

Davis is a coldblooded, Oriental genius attempting to seize control of a Polaris submarine via memory-erasing technology and the manipulation of CIA agent Wagner. Produced for ABC's *Movie of the Week,* but considerably better than standard TV fare.

Davis obviously relishes her chance to be a combination Fu Manchu/Abominable Dr. Phibes.

MAGIC SWORD, THE (1962) C. *Dir.:* Bert I. Gordon. *With:* Gary Lockwood, Basil Rathbone, Anne Helm. **80 mins.** No rating. Beta, VHS **($49.95).** Video Yesteryear. ★★½
Schlockmeister Gordon's interpretation of the legend of St. George and the dragon is actually a lot of fun, and is certainly the best of the many low-budgeted films he's made. George falls in love with the princess Helene, imprisoned by an evil sorcerer, and goes to free her with the titular weapon. Colorful episodes prevail as the sorcerer plants a series of fantastic obstacles and monsters between the hero and the heroine.

MAKING OF RAIDERS OF THE LOST ARK/GREAT MOVIE STUNTS, THE (1981) C. *With:* Harrison Ford, Steven Spielberg, George Lucas. **58 mins.** No rating. Beta, VHS **($55.95);** Laser **($29.95);** CED **($19.98).** Paramount. ★★★
This interesting documentary follows the shooting of *Raiders*, comparing the film with early serials and its stunts with the derring-do of ages past. All of the primaries are interviewed and give interesting comments. The real value of this package, however, lies in its focus on Spielberg's directorial techniques, showing him choreographing action like a fan who's already seen the finished film a thousand times.

MAKING OF STAR WARS/SP-FX—THE EMPIRE STRIKES BACK, THE (1980) C. *With:* George Lucas, Mark Hamill, John Dykstra, narrated by William Conrad. **98 mins.** No rating. Beta, VHS **($39.98);** Laser **($29.98);** CED **($19.98).** CBS/Fox. ★★
The shooting of this now classic, big-budget space opera is interesting, but not extraordinarily so. The best footage is devoted to Dykstra's special effects unit's filming of the climactic assault on the Death Star. Its biggest failure is its inability to communicate the magic which Lucas was able to exercise over this chancy, multi-unit production, pulling the pieces together into a glorious whole.

MAKING OF SUPERMAN/SUPERMAN II, THE (1982) C. *With:* Christopher Reeve, Marlon Brando, Richard Donner, Richard Lester. **120 mins.** No rating. Beta, VHS **($59.95).** USA. ★★★
A nice double feature covering the filming of the first two

Superman features. It's not very frank about the well-documented difficulties behind the productions but nevertheless contains items of interest. The directorial techniques of Donner and his replacement Lester are both featured, but are downplayed in favor of the constantly wisecracking, seemingly insecure Reeve and coverage of the special effects units. Offers a unique look at Brando wandering about on the set between takes.

MAN WHO FELL TO EARTH, THE (1976) C. *Dir.:* Nicolas Roeg. *With:* David Bowie, Rip Torn, Candy Clark. **118 mins.** Rated R. Beta, VHS **($64.95)**; Laser **($29.95)**; CED **($29.95)**. RCA/Columbia. ★★★★
An alien comes to Earth in the hope of saving his dying, drought-plagued planet. After becoming fabulously wealthy from his scientific inventions, he finds himself corrupted by alcohol and human attachments. Bowie is excellent in his film debut, and is perfectly supported by Roeg's typically eccentric and multidimensional direction. Already established as a SF classic, its original 140-minute length (shown on cable TV) remains, sadly, unreleased to video.

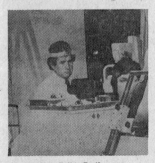

The Man Who Fell to Earth   The Man Who Wasn't There

MAN WHO WASN'T THERE, THE (1983) C. *Dir.:* Bruce Malmuth. *With:* Steve Guttenberg, Lisa Langlois, Art Hindle. **111 mins.** Rated R. Beta, VHS **($59.95)**. Paramount. ★
A moronic, contemporary comedy that uses H. G. Wells' invisibility concept as a way for Guttenberg to peek into girls' showers and to present the nude Langlois seemingly making love to herself. Shown in theaters in very bad 3-D. If the star of the movie doesn't show up, why should you?

MAROONED (1969) C. *Dir.:* John Sturges. *With:* Gregory Peck, Gene Hackman, Richard Crenna. **134 mins.** Rated G. Beta, VHS **($59.95).** RCA/Columbia. ★★½

This semi-documentary of the Apollo space mission trapped in orbit became something of a *cause célèbre,* à la *The China Syndrome,* when the same thing occurred in real life. The worries of the astronaut's wives and the frustrations at Mission Control keep the story at an uncomfortably fierce boil. Superbly realistic but, if anything, the film suffers from its own scrupulousness and plays more dryly than it should.

MARTIAN CHRONICLES I, II, & III, THE (1979) C. *Dir.:* Michael Anderson. *With:* Rock Hudson, Gayle Hunnicutt, Bernie Casey. **120 mins.** each. No rating. Beta, VHS **($59.95 each).** USA. ★★

This made-for-TV adaptation of Ray Bradbury's classic doesn't seem to have recognized the ambitiousness of its own task. Earth's first expedition to Mars uncovers the existence of a powerful, telepathic race that adopts the forms and thought patterns of invading Earthlings in order to protect their planet. Director Anderson, responsible for many an SF bomb *(Logan's Run, Orca, Murder by Phone),* translates this epic material into his longest yawn yet.

MASTER OF THE WORLD (1961) C. *Dir.:* William Witney. *With:* Vincent Price, Charles Bronson, Henry Hull. **104 mins.** No rating. Beta, VHS **($59.95).** Warner. ★★½

This better-than-average SF-fantasy is adapted from Jules Verne's *Robur the Conqueror,* but takes its cue from *20,000 Leagues Under the Sea,* as two men and a woman are abducted by ingenious Price's fabulous air sub, the Albatross. Like Nemo, Robur is homicidally anti-militant, bombing 19th-century battleships from the skies, with Price communicating his internal struggles quite well. Speculative, adventurous fun scripted by Richard Matheson.

MEDUSA TOUCH, THE (1978) C. *Dir.:* Jack Gold. *With:* Richard Burton, Lee Remick, Lino Ventura. **109 mins.** Rated PG. Beta, VHS **($59.95).** CBS/Fox. ★★

Burton is a bedridden, telepathic novelist who can no longer control the disasters resulting from his intellectual aggression. Remick is assigned to psychiatrically audit his case, which is strewn with psychically slain corpses, and to find a means of diverting his energies. Not very well made, but the film does manage some intriguing comments on the symbiotic nature of destruction and creation.

MEGAFORCE (1982) C. *Dir.:* Hal Needham. *With:* Barry Bostwick, Persis Khambatta, Michael Beck. **99 mins.** Rated PG. Beta, VHS **($59.95);** CED **($19.98).** CBS/Fox. ★

Bostwick is Ace Hunter, a futuristic stunt cop who marshalls an arsenal of unimaginative weapons and vehicles in a shamelessly derivative SF-action piece. Even more disappointing than the film's reliance on car chases and spectacular crashes is the primitivism of every single character. The future is depicted as a paradise where man won't have to think, as long as he can drive and shoot.

METALSTORM (1983) C. *Dir.:* Charles Band. *With:* Jeffrey Byron, Mike Preston, Tim Thomerson. **84 mins.** Rated PG. Beta Hi-Fi, VHS **($59.95);** Laser **($29.98);** CED **($29.98).** MCA. ★

When a miner is killed on the planet Lemuria for digging unusual crystals, a Peacemaking Ranger is assigned to track down his murderers, the cyborg Baal, and the diabolical Jared-Syn. The film subscribes to the incorrect notion that all a SF production requires is a plethora of goofy-sounding words and funny-looking characters. Jared-Syn is *never* destroyed, by the way; he just disappears into a sequel that, let us pray, will never be made.

METEOR (1979) C. *Dir.:* Ronald Neame. *With:* Sean Connery, Natalie Wood, Karl Malden. **105 mins.** Rated PG. Beta, VHS **($59.95).** Warner. ★½

After rescuing Earth from *The Swarm,* Irwin Allen placed the planet on a hopeless, star-studded collision course with a gigantic asteroid! Spectacle has never been more pathetic than in this last feature-length gasp from the Master of Disaster, which reaches an apex of absurdity when America and the Soviet Union put away their ideologies to mutually blast the big rock with nuclear weapons. Novelist Anthony Burgess initiated this project but left for reasons that needn't be explained; undaunted, Allen went on to produce TV-movies like *And Millions Will Die!*

METROPOLIS (1926) B/W. *Dir.:* Fritz Lang. *With:* Rudolf Klein-Rogge, Brigitte Helm, Alfred Abel. **131 mins.** Silent. No rating. Beta, VHS **($69.96).** Video Yesteryear. ★★★★

A silent German classic about an industrialized future society presided over by ivory tower executives, with its overbearing machinery constantly attended by an overworked proletariat. The son of the city's designer joins a rebellious underground movement to overthrow his father's kind. Eventually the two sides unite against a flood threatening to destroy all their dreams. This early SF production still gleams with modernity and intelligence; this is *not* the new-wave musical concocted from original footage by Giorgio Moroder in 1984.

MIGHTY JOE YOUNG (1949) B/W. *Dir.:* Ernest Schoedsack. *With:* Terry Moore, Ben Johnson, Robert Armstrong. **94 mins.** No rating. Beta, VHS **($34.95).** Nostalgia Merchant. ★★★½

A show business mogul imports a giant ape and its teenage paramour to New York from Africa. (Sound familiar?) While the producer/director team of the original *King Kong* are clearly exploiting former glories here, the result has survived as one of the screen's most accomplished fantasies. The climax at the burning orphanage is a high point in the history of special effects.

MISSION GALACTICA: THE CYLON ATTACK (1980) C. *Dir.:* Vince Edwards. *With:* Lorne Greene, Lloyd Bridges, Anne Lockhart. **94 mins.** Rated G. Beta, VHS **($39.95).** MCA. ★★

This feature-length condensation of two hour-long episodes of an ABC teleseries follows the Galactica crew's retribution against its Cylon foes for damage done to planet Earth. Only special effects aficionados will find much of interest here, as it is the sole ingredient that breaks out of the small-screen mold. A third *Galactica* feature, *Galactica III: Conquest of the Earth,* covers the same ground.

MISTER SUPERINVISIBLE (1973) C. *Dir.:* Anthony Dawson (Antonio Margheriti). *With:* Dean Jones, Ingeborg Schoener, Peter Carsten. **91 mins.** Beta, VHS **($49.95).** K-Tel. ★★

Scientist Jones is conducting an experiment to discover a cure for the common cold but instead finds a formula for invisibility. This Disneyesque story is fair enough, but its Italian production has little of Disney's gloss or charm, and the dubbing is atrocious. Has there been an original invisible man film since the first?

MONSTER A GO-GO (1965) C. *Dir.:* Herschell Gordon Lewis and Bill Rebane. *With:* June Travis, Phil Morton, George Perry. **70**

mins. No rating. Beta, VHS **($39.95)**. VCI. ★

On his return to earth, an astronaut is transformed into a 10-foot tall monster (Henry Hite). This is actually Rebane's film, which famed goremeister Lewis completed with transition shots and an annoying narration. Not even Lewis liked the film, a fact confirmed by his advertising slogan: "You've Never Seen a Picture Like This—Thank Goodness!"

MONSTER X. See GODZILLA VS. MONSTER ZERO.

MOTHRA (1961) C. *Dir.:* Inoshiro Honda. *With:* Frankie Sakai, Hiroshi Koizumi, Emi and Yumi Itoh. **100 mins.** No rating. Beta, VHS **($59.95).** RCA/Columbia. ★★½

The sudden appearance of a giant moth in Tokyo leads to the discovery of an island civilization which worships it, as well as two thimble-sized sisters who can calm the creature with song. There is a lot of amusing, semi-serious espionage surrounding the abduction of the sisters, and not as much wholesale city-stomping as in Honda's other films. A delightfully demure little fantasy with a fine exotic flavor.

MURDER BY PHONE (1980) C. *Dir.:* Michael Anderson. *With:* Richard Chamberlain, John Houseman, Sara Botsford. **79 mins.** Rated R. Beta, VHS **($39.98).** Warner. ★★

The preposterous concept of an electronics genius sending fatal, electronic impulses through the telephone system—making neon of his enemies—somehow evolves into one of Anderson's few watchable endeavors. Chamberlain (clearly just collecting a paycheck) is the bearded, environmental troubleshooter whose awareness of the situation is pooh-poohed as paranoia by officials he's fingered in the past. Hollow performances and shallow direction mar an otherwise intriguing film.

MURDER BY TELEVISION (1935) B/W. *Dir.:* Clifford Sandforth. *With:* Bela Lugosi, June Collyer, Huntley Gordon. **55 mins.** Beta, VHS **($39.95).** Video Yesteryear. ★★

A standard mystery from the early talkies era distinguished by its shockingly timely murder weapon: a television signal converted by an electronics genius into a deadly ray. Not good, but certainly prophetic.

MUTANT. See FORBIDDEN WORLD.

MYSTERIANS, THE (1957) C. *Dir.:* Inoshiro Honda. *With:* Kenji Sahara, Yumi Shirakawa, Momoko Koichi. **85 mins.** No rating. Beta, VHS **($54.95).** VCI. ★★★

This silly film has folk from the planet Mysterioid ravaging Earth with gigantic robots and death rays so that they may make off (and later make *out*) with its women. Amazingly, the subject matter is handled with unusual verve. Honda and his effects man Eiji Tsuburaya accomplished their best work here, following the production of the original *Godzilla: King of the Monsters.* It's colorful, stylish, (but let us not forget) *juvenile* fun.

MYSTERIOUS DOCTOR SATAN, THE (1940) B/W. *Dir.:* William Witney and John English. *With:* Eduardo Ciannelli, Robert Wilcox, Ella Neal. **250 mins.** No rating. Beta, VHS **($N/A).** Nostalgia Merchant. ★★½

Dr. Satan (Ciannelli) needs a remote control device before he can dominate Earth with his evil robot, but the heroic Copperhead—a man in a copper whole-head mask—keeps getting in his way. Pretty much your standard Hollywood serial, but it's well paced thanks to the work of the Witney-English team (see *King of the Rocket Men*).

MYSTERIOUS ISLAND (1961) C. *Dir.:* Cy Endfield. *With:* Michael Callan, Joan Greenwood, Herbert Lom. **101 mins.** No rating. Beta, VHS **($59.95);** Laser **($29.95);** CED **($19.98).** RCA/ Columbia. ⬜® ★★★½

A group of convicts escaping prison via balloon are blown off course by a storm to an uncharted island teeming with gigantic (and, fortunately, always edible) birds, bees, and crabs. This is one of Ray Harryhausen's most satisfying stop-motion animation showcases, magnificently enhanced by thrilling Bernard Herrmann score. Lom appears in the role of Captain Nemo just in time to save the day.

NAVY VS. THE NIGHT MONSTERS, THE (1966) C. *Dir.:* Michael Hoey. *With:* Mamie Van Doren, Bobby Van, Billy Gray. **90 mins.** No rating. Beta, VHS **($N/A).** Paragon. ★½

An Antarctic naval base (where the dress code says, "short sleeves") is terrorized by walking, acid-bleeding, strangling vine creatures bent on invasion. Never has a more preposterous premise been coupled with such an equally preposterous cast, but any SF film with the late, great Bobby Van is entertainment *guaran-*

teed. One of the best bad films of its kind in color. (aka THE NIGHT CRAWLERS.)

NEVERENDING STORY, THE (1984) C. *Dir.:* Wolfgang Petersen. *With:* Barret Oliver, Noah Hathaway, Moses Gunn. **94 mins.** Rated G. Beta, VHS **($79.95);** Laser **($34.98);** CED **($29.98).** Warner. ★★½

A bullied boy, whose mother's death has left him with a penchant for fantasy, reads a book that physically involves him in an adventure in the land of Fantasia, where he rescues a princess from "the dreaded Nothing." This is one of the most nakedly Freudian films ever made, with Fantasia itself a blatant maternal substitute full of womb-like caves and full-breasted sphinxes. A preachy film with strong visual imagination and rather astonishing sound effects.

NEXT ONE, THE (1982) C. *Dir.:* Nico Mastorakis. *With:* Adrienne Barbeau, Kier Dullea, Peter Hobbs. **105 mins.** Rated PG. Beta, VHS **($69.95).** Vestron. ★★

A cross between *The Man Who Fell to Earth* and *King of Kings* (if you can imagine that), this attractive film opens with Dullea waking up with mysterious gifts of prescience and intuition. The final explanation is either blasé, haunting, or offensive, depending on one's religious orientation. Gorgeous scenery and one of Barbeau's rare, soft characterizations.

NIGHT BEAST (1983) C. *Dir.:* Don Dohler. *With:* Tom Griffith, Jaimie Zemarel, George Stover. **90 mins.** Rated R. Beta, VHS **($34.95).** Paragon. ★

This amateurish production acts as a lurid, gratuitously violent parody of *E.T.,* with a stranded, laser-wielding alien ravaging the town of Perry Hill. A lot of blood, bad acting, and scratched-celluloid laser blasts. Cast member Stover, one of the monster's many victims, supplements his acting career by publishing the fanzine *Cinemacabre.*

NIGHT CRAWLERS, THE. See THE NAVY VS. THE NIGHT MONSTERS.

NIGHT GAMES (1980) C. *Dir.:* Roger Vadim. *With:* Cindy Pickett, Joanna Cassidy, Barry Primus. **100 mins.** Rated R. Beta, VHS **($69.95);** Laser, CED **($29.95).** Embassy. ★½

The weak, narcissistic story of Pickett's wandering sexual imagination during her husband's absence is of marginal interest as she becomes tangled in (real or imagined?) ritual visits from a plume-masked, male lover. The situation arouses the viewer's imagination without satisfying it, resulting in a very disappointing resolution. Pickett and Cassidy make an otherwise flat-looking film attractive.

99 AND 44/100% DEAD (1974) C. *Dir.:* John Frankenheimer. *With:* Richard Harris, Chuck Connors, Bradford Dillman. **98 mins.** Rated R. Beta, VHS **($59.95).** CBS/Fox. ★★

Not your usual gangster film. This movie is staged in a bizarre milieu that is equal parts comic book, pop art, and alternate universe, where those with aversions to violence have moved underground. The sewers are full of albino alligators, the bay has more stiffs than the city morgue (a wonderful shot), and the city is in the hands of two syndicates warring for the territory. It could've been better, but this uneven SF-action film is too energetic and unusual to deny a passing mark.

984—Prisoner of the Future   1990: The Bronx Warriors

984—PRISONER OF THE FUTURE (1984) C. *Dir.:* Tibor Takacs. *With:* Don Francks and Stephen Markel. **70 mins.** No rating. Beta, VHS **($59.95).** VCL. ★½

A low-budget, dystopian parable about former executive Markel who is imprisoned and tortured in a futuristic complex run by dogmatic followers of "The Movement." The film's premise, which has America turning toward gross intellectualism, Is unbelievable and any similarity to TV's *The Prisoner* (see review) is superficial and flattering. Has no real point to make.

1990: THE BRONX WARRIORS (1983) C. *Dir.:* Enzo G. Castellari. *With:* Vic Morrow, Fred Williamson, Christopher Connelly. **86 mins.** Rated R. Beta, VHS **($59.95)**. Media. ★

This worthless Italian rip-off of *Escape From New York* and *The Warriors* envisions a future Bronx ruled by youth gangs in absurd costumes and rollerskates. An unrelieved wallow in macho posturing, with some of the most unnecessary dialogue ever filmed.

NUTTY PROFESSOR, THE (1963) C. *Dir.:* Jerry Lewis. *With:* Jerry Lewis, Stella Stevens, Del Moore. **107 mins.** No rating. Beta, VHS **($49.95)**; Laser **($29.95)**; CED **($19.98)**. Paramount. ★★★½

Lewis is the college chemistry professor Julius Kelp, whose shyness prompts the development of a health tonic/macho potion. As a result, he is transformed into Buddy Love, a repulsive package of the least desirable male qualities. Long acknowledged as Lewis' only real masterpiece, the film works as brilliant comedy and as a serious excavation of its director-star's complex persona (with a sequel now in the works). Fabulously colorful, with Stevens and supporting group of Lewis regulars at their best.

O LUCKY MAN! (1973) C. *Dir.:* Lindsay Anderson. *With:* Malcolm McDowell, Helen Mirren, Rachel Roberts. **173 mins.** Rated R. Beta, VHS **($59.95)**. Warner. ★★★★

McDowell plays an enterprising, opportunistic coffee salesman whose travels throughout the British Isles (in a magical, shielding suit) form a most brutal and brilliant education in human nature. His sales trips are punctuated with unnerving, adventurous tangents, including imprisonment in a base where Cold War spies are tortured and a stay in a hospital where men's heads are being transplanted onto sheep. Alan Price contributes one of the movies' all-time great scores to this semi-sequel to Anderson's *If. . . .*

ON THE BEACH (1959) B/W. *Dir.:* Stanley Kramer. *With:* Gregory Peck, Ava Gardner, Fred Astaire. **134 mins.** No rating. Beta, VHS **($59.98)**; CED **($39.98)**. CBS/Fox. ★★★

The drifting, nuclear essence of WWIII spreads to the antipodal regions of the globe, where it is awaited by Australia and an American submarine stationed in its waters. This starkly monochromatic film is excellently photograpned (an early assignment for Giuseppe Rotunno), but is thematically blunted by Kramer's ham-handed message orientation. Astaire's superlative work in his first nonmusical role is the major highlight of this adaptation of Nevil Shute's bestseller.

ONE MILLION B.C. (1940) B/W. *Dir.:* Hal Roach and Hal Roach, Jr. *With:* Victor Mature, Lon Chaney, Jr., Carole Landis. **80 mins.** No rating. Beta, VHS **($N/A).** Nostalgia Merchant. ★★½

The first feature to dramatize prehistoric life follows the odyssey of Mature, a tribesman from a carnivorous group, after he is ousted for defying leader Chaney. After a Christ-like trek across the desert, he encounters a calm-natured vegetarian tribe in whose company he confronts numerous giant lizards and, finally, his own people. For his first major role, Chaney hoped to follow in his father's footsteps and wear his own makeup, but the Makeup Artists Union wouldn't allow it.

ORPHEUS (1950) B/W. *Dir.:* Jean Cocteau. *With:* Jean Marais, Maria Dea, Maria Casares. **95 mins.** No rating. Subtitled. Beta, VHS **($49.95).** Video Yesteryear. ★★★½

Cocteau's contemporary interpretation of the Orpheus myth depicts the character as a poet of overwhelming popularity, whose beloved Eurydice is abducted by a mysterious otherworldly woman and taken behind a bedroom mirror into Hell. Orpheus must descend into the realm to save her, but her rescue is only possible if he does not look into her eyes. This entrancing, splendid fantasy contains some unforgettable sights—the motorcycle-straddling servants of Death, Cocteau's simple yet stunning special effects—and has dated only in terms of its literary elegance.

OUTLAND (1981) C. *Dir.:* Peter Hyams. *With:* Sean Connery, Frances Sternhagen, Peter Boyle, James B. Sikking. **109 mins.** Rated R. Beta, VHS **($64.95);** Laser **($29.98);** CED **($19.98).** Warner. ★★

Field marshall Connery traces a high suicide rate on a space station to the use of an illicit government-supplied drug which allegedly decreases stress but actually causes insurmountable depression. The intriguing idea of dramatizing the contamination of a once pure frontier drowns in cheap (not to mention out of place) scare tactics, illogical science, and laser shoot-'em-up sequences that transcend thoughtlessness. Some have noted similarities to *High Noon*, but we have a suspicion that this flattering comparison began in the film's PR kit.

PARTS: THE CLONUS HORROR (1978) C. *Dir.:* Robert S. Fiveson. *With:* Tim Donnelly, Dick Sargent, Paulette Breen. **90 mins.** Rated R. Beta, VHS **($59.95).** Catalina. ★★½

A low-budget potboiler about an evil organization's plan to replace key figures in the government and military with cloned pawns. The hero is actually one of the clones himself, imbued with the same reservations about the takeover plot that his original would have had. This puts a neat twist on the movie which, coupled with some inventive energy on the part of director Fiveson, leads to a much better picture than might be expected.

THE PEACE GAME. See THE GLADIATORS.

PEOPLE THAT TIME FORGOT, THE (1977) C. *Dir.:* Kevin Connor. *With:* Doug McClure, Patrick Wayne, Sara Douglas. **90 mins.** Rated PG. Beta, VHS **($69.95).** Embassy. ★★

The sequel to *The Land That Time Forgot* has the missing explorer McClure traced to a prison of forgotten souls on an exotic, dangerous island. The third and final picture in Amicus' crummy Edgar Rice Burroughs/Doug McClure series is a marginal improvement over its forerunners, having adequate special effects, an interesting cast (John Wayne's son, David Bowie protégé Dana Gillespie, Dave "Darth Vader" Prowse), and shots deliberately composed around celebrated fantasy illustrations.

PHANTOM EMPIRE, THE (1935) B/W. *Dir.:* Otto Brower and Breezy Reeves Eason. *With:* Gene Autry, Frankie Darro, Smiley Burnette. **Approx. 245 mins.** No rating. Beta, VHS **($99.95).** MCA. ★★

This, the downright weirdest serial ever concocted, pits the "singing cowboy" Autry against an underground civilization (Murania) bent on disrupting the harmony at Radio Ranch! The sight of cowboys crossing swords with evil robots and the sound of country-western songs being sung at the earth's core can be enjoyed only here and in the feature-length edition, *Radio Ranch*.

PHANTOM TOLLBOOTH, THE (1969) C. *Dir.:* Chuck Jones, Abe Levitow, and Dave Monahan. *With:* Butch Patrick. **90 mins.** Rated G. Beta, VHS **($49.95);** CED **($29.95).** MGM/UA. ★★★

A little-seen animated feature (with a live-action prologue and epilogue) based on Norman Juster's children's book about a bored child who awakens to the joys of living after a fantasy adventure in a word-woven wonderland. It isn't noticeably didactic, just clever enough to have another dimension of meaning for the benefit of those adults who take the time to watch. It's the only feature-length project by Jones, the most acclaimed director of the old Warner Brothers cartoons, and one of the most enjoyably intellectual filmmakers of our century.

PHASE IV (1974) C. *Dir.:* Saul Bass. *With:* Nigel Davenport, Lynne Frederick, Michael Murphy. **83 mins.** Rated PG. Beta, VHS **($39.95);** Laser **($29.95).** Paramount. ★★★

Desertbound scientists establish communication with an intelligent strain of ants and become unwittingly involved in a tussle for their specific supremacy. The only feature directed to date by the renowned title designer Bass is unquestionably attractive and intelligent, but prefers to give too little information rather than too much. Not a satisfying film, but a worthwhile frustration with a superb "sound sculpture" score by Stomu Yamashta.

PHENOMENAL AND THE TREASURE OF TUTANKAMEN (1984) C. *Dir.:* Roger Rockefeller (Ruggero Deodato). *With:* Maura Nicola Parenti, Lucretia Love, Gordon Mitchell. **91 mins.** No rating. Beta, VHS **($49.95).** Wizard. ★★

Masked superhero Phenomenal (spelled "Fenomenal" on screen) tries to recover the golden mask-piece of King Tut's tomb, which is supernaturally causing the deaths of its many abductors. This fantasy-adventure made in France by Italians as a salute to the silent fantasies of Louis Feuillade (*Fantomas, Judex,* etc.) is directed with intelligence, but is low on charm. The package art is targeted towards children but the film includes a somewhat revealing fist fight between Phenomenal and a bunch of crooks in a ladies' sauna.

PHILADELPHIA EXPERIMENT, THE (1984) C. *Dir.:* Stewart Raffill. *With:* Michael Paré, Nancy Allen, Bobby Di Cicco, Eric Christmas. **102 mins.** Rated PG. Beta, VHS **($79.95).** Thorn EMI. ★★★

Based on an alleged 1943 Naval experiment which successfully rendered a battleship radar-invisible, this film takes the premise one step further by having the test backfire, making the ship completely invisible and hurtling crewmen Paré and Di Cicco ahead into 1984. Good effects, situations, and characters throughout the film make this a tremendous improvement over the director's previous release, *Ice Pirates*. The scenes of Paré discovering elements of 1984 (not to mention intimacy with Allen) bear a strong similarity to those of alien Jeff Bridges in executive producer John Carpenter's subsequent success, *Starman*.

PLAN 9 FROM OUTER SPACE (1959) B/W. *Dir.:* Edward D. Wood, Jr. *With:* Bela Lugosi, Dudley Manlove, Tor Johnson, Vampira. **78 mins.** No rating. Beta, VHS **($39.95).** Nostalgia Merchant. ★½

Aliens dressed in leftover costumes from a King Arthur picture invade Earth in whizzing hubcaps, hoping to conquer the planet by reviving its dead. Everything that *can* go wrong with this SF-horror embarrassment *does*—we go from day to night to day while a car drives down a single street, a cardboard tombstone gets kicked over (no second takes here), and the film's star died two days into production (note the delicacy with which he is replaced in the story). There are worse movies, even more enjoyably bad movies, but this is the one everybody knows about and wants to see with their own eyes.

PLANET OF THE APES (1968) C. *Dir.:* Franklin Schaffner. *With:* Charlton Heston, Kim Hunter, Maurice Evans. **112 mins.** Rated PG. Beta, VHS **($59.98);** CED **($19.98).** CBS/Fox. ★★★

Rod Serling was one of the screenwriters of this big-budget SF-adventure and, while based on a Pierre Boulle novel, it recycles a number of his old *Twilight Zone* plot twists. Heston and fellow astronauts land on an alien planet ruled by talking apes, where all men are mute and reduced to simian levels of society. Superb ensemble acting and top-drawer direction combine in a film of integrity, conscience, and muscle; it far outshines its many sequels.

POPEYE (1980) C. *Dir.:* Robert Altman. *With:* Robin Williams, Shelley Duvall, Ray Walston. **114 mins.** Rated PG. Beta, VHS **($29.95);** Laser **($29.98);** CED **($19.98).** Paramount. ★★★

The bottle-armed sailor Popeye rows into the port town of Sweethaven looking for his long-lost Pappy and finds love, family, and home. Altman's live-action interpretation of E.C. Segar's enduring comic-strip characters is simply a joy, although a controversial one, with every bit of casting an absolute coup. Not a cartoon comedy, but a beguilingly low-key musical about presumably real characters, or at least about universal emotions.

PRISONER, THE: ARRIVAL (1968) C. *Dir.:* Don Chaffey. *With:* Patrick McGoohan, Guy Doleman, Paul Eddington. **50 mins.** No rating, Beta, VHS **($39.95).** Maljack. ★★★½
  Episode 1 of series: Gives new meaning to the lyric, "They've given you a number/and taken away your name." McGoohan resigns from the secret service and is promptly taken into custody by The Village, a deceptively placid community determined to drain him of classified information. He is renamed Number 6 and is introduced to life and death, Village-style. A brilliant espionage idea, packaged as uncommonly intelligent SF.

The Prisoner   The Prisoner

PRISONER, THE: THE CHIMES OF BIG BEN (1968) C. *Dir.:* Don Chaffey. *With:* Patrick McGoohan, Leo McKern, Nadia Gray. **50 mins.** No rating. Beta, VHS **($39.95).** Maljack. ★★★
  Episode 2 of series: Number 6 becomes involved with a new Villager, also an abducted agent, who involves him in a complex and suspenseful escape plan. This segment marks McKern's first appearance as Number 2, The Village's presiding manipulator of actions. A fine script and some tender interaction between McGoohan and Gray make this episode quite enjoyable.

PRISONER, THE: A, B, AND C (1968) C. *Dir.:* Pat Jackson (Patrick McGoohan). *With:* Patrick McGoohan, Katherine Kath, Colin Gordon. **50 mins.** No rating. Beta, VHS **($39.95).** Maljack. ★★★½

Episode 3 of series: One of the most satisfying and experimental episodes, with Number 6's dreams of being investigated in the hopes of finding the reason behind his resignation. The title refers to three characters from Number 6's past, all of whom can be inserted into his dream and artificially manipulated. Gordon is excellent as a nervous, ulcer-ridden Number 2.

PRISONER, THE: FREE FOR ALL (1968) C. *Dir.:* Patrick McGoohan. *With:* Patrick McGoohan, Eric Portman, Rachel Herbert. **50 mins.** No rating. Beta, VHS **($39.95).** Maljack. ★★★
Episode 4 of series: Number 6's curiosity about how authority is obtained in The Village traps him in a political race for the office of Number 2. A vitriolic parody/exposé of the democratic process with a fairly violent denouement.

PRISONER, THE: THE SCHIZOID MAN (1968) C. *Dir.:* Pat Jackson (Patrick McGoohan). *With:* Patrick McGoohan, Jane Merrow, Anton Rogers. **50 mins.** No rating. Beta, VHS **($39.95).** Maljack. ★★★
Episode 5 of series: The Village tries to force Number 6 to reveal his secrets by causing him to doubt his own identity, changing his appearance and personal traits, and introducing an identical twin. The episode keeps the viewer equally unbalanced, unfolding like a deceptive shell game played with human brains. Merrow is memorable as Number 6's neighbor, a psychic with whom he shares a mental link.

PRISONER, THE: THE GENERAL (1968) C. *Dir.:* Peter Graham Scott. *With:* Patrick McGoohan, Colin Gordon, John Castle. **50 mins.** No rating. Beta, VHS **($39.95).** Maljack. ★★
Episode 6 of series: The inhabitants of The Village are given compulsory, televised education courses—taught in a split second by a beam sent through their eyes. The implications of brainwashing are mild, inconsequential, and not nearly as potent as those in the preceding chapter, "The Schizoid Man." Ends disappointingly.

PRISONER, THE: MANY HAPPY RETURNS (1968) C. *Dir.:* Joseph Serf. *With:* Patrick McGoohan, Patrick Cargill, Georgina Cookson. **50 mins.** No rating. Beta, VHS **($39.95).** Maljack. ★★★★
Episode 7 of series: Number 6 awakens to find The Village completely deserted, and takes advantage of the situation to col-

lect proof of his adventure, build a raft, and return to England. One of the series' greatest stories, the first half unfolding entirely without dialogue, lends valuable insights into McGoohan's character, his resourcefulness, and his worth as a secret agent. The resolution is cleverly telegraphed, and its fulfillment of our anticipations is delicious.

PRISONER, THE: DANCE OF THE DEAD (1968) C. *Dir.:* Don Chaffey. *With:* Patrick McGoohan, Mary Morris. **50 mins.** No rating. Beta, VHS **($39.95).** Maljack. ★★★
Episode 8 of series: Number 6 meets a comrade from his former existence and becomes entangled in a hideous scheme to convince the outside world of his own death. A bizarre, unsettling episode that culminates at a masked ball suggestive of a tier in Dante's Inferno.

PRISONER, THE: DO NOT FORSAKE ME OH MY DARLING (1968) C. *Dir.:* Pat Jackson. *With:* Patrick McGoohan, Zena Walker, Nigel Stock. **50 mins.** No rating. Beta, VHS **($39.95).** Maljack. ★★★½
Episode 9 of series: Number 6's mind transmigrates into the body of a free Village accomplice, with another actor playing McGoohan's role for most of the show. Through this man we learn quite a bit about the pre-Village life of Number 6—we meet his fiancée, her father (a higher-up in his former work), and their presumptions of his present whereabouts—with fascinating, even poignant results. McGoohan directed under his usual pseudonym. The episode is reminiscent of the French *nouvelle vague* films of its day, and is the first diversion from the show's structure (including a pre-credits scene that makes you wonder if you're watching the right program!).

PRISONER, THE: IT'S YOUR FUNERAL (1968) C. *Dir.:* Robert Asher. *With:* Patrick McGoohan, Derren Nesbitt, Annette Andre. **50 mins.** No rating. Beta, VHS **($39.95).** Maljack. ★★
Episode 10 of series: An amusing vignette on the subject of political assassination. Number 6's role seems rather incidental in all this.

PRISONER, THE: CHECKMATE (1968) C. *Dir.:* Don Chaffey. *With:* Patrick McGoohan, Peter Wyngarde, Ronald Radd. **50 mins.** No rating. Beta, VHS **($39.95).** Maljack. ★★★

Episode 11 of series: This clever little story follows the efforts of Number 6 to learn which Villge inhabitants are the prisoners and which are the jailers. Many intriguing moments, notably a chess game played with human pieces, which build to an ironic finale. Wyngarde is excellent as the Mephistophelian Number 2.

PRISONER, THE: LIVING IN HARMONY (1968) C. *Dir.:* David Tomblin. *With:* Patrick McGoohan, Alexis Kanner, Valerie French. **50 mins.** No rating. Beta, VHS **($39.95).** Maljack. ★★★★
Episode 12 of series: The notorious "western" episode, a complex and thematically rich entry which recounts the moral justifications of not wearing a gun for The State. Psychologically and physically violent, with an off-screen rape and murder, it was never aired during the program's initial American network run. Kanner is particularly brilliant as The Kid.

PRISONER, THE: CHANGE OF MIND, A (1968) C. *Dir.:* Joseph Serf. *With:* Patrick McGoohan, John Sharpe, Angela Browne. **50 mins.** No rating. Beta, VHS **($39.95).** Maljack. ★★
Episode 13 of series: A rehash of themes and situations stated in previous episodes, notably *Free for All* and *The Schizoid Man.* Well-acted, but the series was clearly coasting here.

PRISONER, THE: HAMMER INTO ANVIL (1968) C. *Dir.:* Pat Jackson (Patrick McGoohan). *With:* Patrick McGoohan, Patrick Cargill, Victor Maddern. **50 mins.** No rating. Beta, VHS **($39.95).** Maljack. ★★★
Episode 14 of series: Number 6 wages an all out, psychological war against the sadistic and unstable Number 2 (brilliantly portrayed by Cargill) in this very funny, albeit implausible, story. Played to the tune of Bizet's *L'Arlesienne,* this episode contains some of the series' most humorous moments.

PRISONER, THE: THE GIRL WHO WAS DEATH (1968) C. *Dir.:* David Tomblin. *With:* Patrick McGoohan, Justine Lord, Kenneth Griffith. **50 mins.** No rating. Beta, VHS **($39.95).** Maljack. ★★★
Episode 15 of series: Number 6 narrates a spy's version of a fairy tale to the children of The Village, a riotous farce filled with nonsensical events that mirror his disdain for his captors. One of the series' most clever and refreshing story premises, with a particularly fresh ending.

PRISONER, THE: ONCE UPON A TIME (1968) C. *Dir.:* Patrick McGoohan. *With:* Patrick McGoohan, Leo McKern, Angelo Muscat. **50 mins.** No rating. Beta, VHS **($39.95).** Maljack. ★★★★

Episode 16 of series: A remarkable, one-on-one psychodrama between Number 6 and McKern's Number 2. Truth mingles with fiction, providing brilliant insights into the two men. After the fierce confrontation, Number 6 *appears* to have overcome all that has been put in his way....

PRISONER, THE: FALL OUT (1968) C. *Dir.:* Patrick McGoohan. *With:* Patrick McGoohan, Leo McKern, Alexis Kanner. **50 mins.** No rating. Beta, VHS **($39.95).** Maljack. ★★★★

Episode 17, the last of series: Number 6 is the guest of honor in a kangaroo court in an underground cave. The story abandons the realm of fiction in favor of full-fledged allegory, which made many viewers irate when it was first aired. However eccentric, this cryptic and challenging episode is an obvious must for anyone interested in the breadth and depth of fantasy in cinema.

Prisoners of the Lost Universe   Quest for Fire

PRISONERS OF THE LOST UNIVERSE (1982) C. *Dir.:* Terry Marcel. *With:* Kay Lenz. John Saxon, Richard Hatch. **94 mins.** Rated PG. Beta, VHS **($69.95).** VCL. ★

The "lost universe" is a purgatory of failed film elements, and the "prisoners" are a gruff scientist, a female TV science reporter, and a roving electrician. "The prisoners" collide with a collection of half-cocked characters, including a race of glowing-eyed pygmies, a prehistoric man, and the Green Man (a cross between Daniel Boone and a Martian). It's dumb, but this *inspired* stupidity keeps one watching for the next cliché in a seemingly endless chain.

PROVIDENCE (1977) C. *Dir.:* Alain Resnais. *With:* John Gielgud, Dirk Bogarde, Ellen Burstyn, David Warner. **104 mins.** Rated R. Beta, VHS **($59.95).** RCA/Columbia. ★★★★

Dying novelist Gielgud spends a riotous, profane final night of existence in bed, drinking, agonizing with cancer, and mentally amusing himself with pages from a fantasy novel he knows will never be completed. The action within these pages (which is presented to us first, before we realize it is not part of the real story) includes everything from extramarital affairs to bank-robbing werewolves, and feature his own family in a variety of poses and situations that reveal how little this wise man understands them. One of Resnais' best, spearheaded by Gielgud's finest performance.

PURPLE MONSTER STRIKES, THE (1945) B/W. *Dir.:* Spencer Gordon Bennet and Fred C. Brannon. *With:* Dennis Moore, Linda Stirling, Roy Barcroft. **260 mins.** No rating. Beta, VHS **($N/A).** Nostalgia Merchant. ★★

Barcroft is Mota, a costumed, villianous Martian who arrives inside a fully furnished meteor to threaten Earth with devastation. This 15-chapter Republic serial is empty-headed fun, but actually no more than typical of its kind, with the extraterrestrial villiany contested by a costumed hero with the unlikely moniker of the title. The condensed feature version is called *D-Day on Mars*.

QUATERMASS II: ENEMY FROM SPACE (1957) B/W. *Dir.:* Val Guest. *With:* Brian Donlevy, Bryan Forbes, Sydney James. **84 mins.** No rating. Beta, VHS **($54.95).** Corinth. ★★★★

The second film from Nigel Kneale's tetralogy of SF-mysteries about physics professor Quatermass involves the possible extraterrestrial connection between the discovery of gas-emitting meteorites, the theft of Q's blueprints for a proposed moonbase, and those burns on the cheeks of men in high places. Superb writing, direction, and camerawork make this production to British cinema what Don Siegel's *Invasion of the Body Snatchers* was to American. Long withheld from circulation due to Kneale's displeasure with Donlevy's portrayal of his sensitive scientist.

QUEST FOR FIRE (1982) C. *Dir.:* Jean-Jacques Annaud. *With:* Rae Dawn Chong, Everett McGill, Ron Perlman, Nameer El-Kadi. **100 mins.** Rated R. Beta, VHS **($69.98);** Laser **($34.98);** CED **($19.98).** CBS/Fox. ★★★

When a Neanderthal tribe's only torch is doused, three of its men leave on a journey to find a new source of warmth for their loved ones. This ambitious and charming saga follows these surprisingly personable lugs through scary, erotic, and comical encounters with neighboring tribes until they reach their goal (in one of the SF-fantasy cinema's most moving sequences). The grunts of the actors were actually scripted in accordance with ancient language syllables by novelist/linguist Anthony Burgess.

RADAR MEN FROM THE MOON (1952) B/W. *Dir.:* Fred C. Brannon. *With:* George Wallace, Roy Barcroft, Clayton Moore. **260 mins.** No rating. Beta, VHS **($N/A).** Nostalgia Merchant. ★★★

Mostly enjoyable, inspired nonsense, this 12-part Republic serial introduced Commando Cody, Sky Marshall of the Universe—or, frankly, a new character designed to unmothball the costume from *King of the Rocket Men* (see review). Cody's ire is riled by none other than Retik the Moon Menace (Barcroft, the Martian from *The Purple Monster Strikes*), whose atomic artillery is focused on Earth. Camp entertainment at its most overt.

RADIO RANCH (1940) B/W. *Dir.:* Otto Brower and Breezy Reeves Eason. *With:* Gene Autry, Betsy King Ross, Frankie Darro. **80 mins.** No rating. Beta, VHS **($49.95).** Video Yesteryear. ★½

See THE PHANTOM EMPIRE (1935).

RAIDERS OF THE LOST ARK (1981) C. *Dir.:* Steven Spielberg. *With:* Harrison Ford, Karen Allen, John Rhys-Davies, Denholm Elliott. **115 mins.** Rated PG. Beta Hi-Fi, VHS **($39.95);** Laser **($29.95);** CED **($29.95).** Paramount. ▢® ★★★★

This definitive action film is a breathtaking paen to Hollywood cliffhangers, with a new danger engulfing hero Indiana Jones every few minutes, as he represents America against the Nazis in a search for the lost Ark of the Covenant. The climactic unleashing of the artifact's Holy fire is a masterwork of visual-effects ingenuity and dramatic force. The entire cast is at its best in this masterpiece, which was produced by George Lucas, and also represents director Spielberg at the height of his powers.

RED BALLOON, THE/AN OCCURRENCE AT OWL CREEK BRIDGE (1956/62) C & B/W. *Dir.:* Albert Lamourisse and Robert Enrico. *With:* Pascal Lamourisse, Roger Jacquet. **60 mins.** No rating. Beta, VHS **($39.95).** Budget. ★★★★

Raiders of the Lost Ark

The Red Balloon

A terrific double feature of two of the best European shorts of our time. *The Red Balloon* is a delightful story about a lonely French boy befriended by a seemingly alive red balloon. *An Occurrence at Owl Creek Bridge,* based on the classic Ambrose Bierce tale, studies the fantasized escape of a Confederate spy about to be hanged (it was first shown in the U.S. as the final episode of *The Twilight Zone*).

RED DAWN (1984) C. *Dir.:* John Milius. *With:* Patrick Swayze, C. Thomas Howell, Powers Boothe. **114 mins.** Rated PG-13. Beta Hi-Fi, VHS **($79.95)**; CED **($29.98).** MGM/UA. ★★½
A small band of American teens wage guerrilla warfare against Russian/Cuban troops staging an invasion of their midwestern town. Milius gathers some of Hollywood's strongest young talent, but the stark cultural similarities of the actors blur what should have been distinct and championable personalities. The result is an action piece smothered by political and dramatic insensitivity.

REINCARNATION OF PETER PROUD, THE (1975) C. *Dir.:* J. Lee Thompson. *With:* Michael Sarrazin, Jennifer O'Neill, Margot Kidder. **104 mins.** Rated R. Beta, VHS **($N/A).** Vestron. ★½
Sarrazin is a teacher experiencing a recurring nightmare about a violent drowning. He accidentally learns the dream is the memory of his own murder in a previous life. The subsequent investigation results in meeting "his" former wife/murderess and becomes even more complicated when he falls in love with "his" daughter. Based on the okay Max Ehrlich best-seller, the film does have a haunting Jerry Goldsmith score, but not much else.

REPO MAN (1984) C. *Dir.:* Alex Cox. *With:* Emilio Estevez, Harry Dean Stanton, Olivia Barash. **92 mins.** Rated R. Beta Hi-Fi, VHS Hi-Fi **($59.95).** MCA. ★★★½

Estevez plays Otto ("auto," get it?), an L.A. street punk lassoed into a thrilling, rewarding, frightening career as a repo man, or car repossesser. Paid by commission, he sets his sights on retrieving an old Chevy Malibu that will pay $20,000—because it happens to have the decaying, radioactive corpses of four space creatures in its trunk! Film may run out of gas during its climax, but the viewer is exhausted with laughter well before this; a film truly fed up with reality.

RESURRECTION OF ZACHARY WHEELER, THE (1971) C. *Dir.:* Robert Wynn. *With:* Angie Dickinson, Bradford Dillman, Leslie Nielsen. **100 mins.** Rated G. Beta, VHS **($54.95).** VCI. ★★

A reporter follows a presidential candidate to a New Mexico clinic after a near-fatal car accident. There he discovers a malevolent organization which replaces damaged organs with synthetic ones and entire bodies with duplicates, blackmailing their restored patients to gain footholds in government. Released directly to TV, this interesting feature was produced entirely on videotape, which is an irritant to the eyes. Nevertheless, this early cloning tale entertains.

RETURN, THE (1980) C. *Dir.:* Greydon Clark. *With:* Jan-Michael Vincent, Cybill Shepherd, Raymond Burr. **91 mins.** Rated PG. Beta, VHS **($59.95).** Thorn EMI. ★

An unwatchable, addle-brained SF concoction about how a miner and two children abducted by a UFO are affected by the adventure, and how its return 20 years later changes their lives. Never shown in theaters, this film is indeed best suited to a medium with an on-off switch.

ROAD WARRIOR, THE (1981) C. *Dir.:* George Miller. *With:* Mel Gibson, Bruce Spence, Emil Minty. **95 mins.** Rated R. Beta, VHS **($69.95);** Laser **($29.98);** CED **($29.98).** Warner. ★★★★

This sequel to *Mad Max* is staged even further in the future, with Max helping an oil-producing commune move its precious fuel from their failing fortress to a new locale while fighting off outrageous packs of demonic punks. This riveting and poignant SF-action piece takes its cue from the western classic *Shane,* lending the film a handsome, mythic stance. A minor masterpiece of the genre, made on a miniscule budget with all the grace and style of a megamillions Spielberg extravaganza.

ROBOT MONSTER (1953) B/W. *Dir.:* Phil Tucker. *With:* George Nader, Gregory Moffett, Claudia Barrett. **63 mins.** No rating. Beta, VHS **($45.00).** Festival. ★½

Ro-Man, an alien emissary from a planet which has successfully conquered nearly all of Earth, lives in a cave, communicates with home via a bubble machine, and stalks the last six "hu-mans" left on the planet. Shot in less than a week for under $20,000, this is one of the most sublimely incompetent SF films, and a wonderful index to the layman's perception of the genre (i.e., Ro-Man never "thinks again," he "recalculates"!). When modern-day Earth is destroyed in the final moments, we see stock footage of dying dinosaurs!

ROCKET TO THE MOON. See CAT WOMEN OF THE MOON.

ROCKETSHIP X-M (SPECIAL EDITION) (1950) B/W. *Dir.:* Kurt Neumann. *With:* Lloyd Bridges, Osa Massen, Hugh O'Brien. **77 mins.** No rating. Beta, VHS **($29.95).** Nostalgia Merchant. ★★½

This low-budget, fairly good feature was rushed to theaters to beat "the first serious space movie" *Destination Moon*. X-M, or "Xpedition Moon," is bound for the moon (hence its name) until a meteor shower and other complications throw the rocket off-course, causing a forced landing on Mars. The downbeat finale was bold for its day, and the film's video release contains red-tinted Mars sequences and some new (1978) special effects which will only confuse the viewer and detract from its curiosity value.

RODAN (1956) C. *Dir.:* Inoshiro Honda. *With:* Kenji Sahara, Yumi Shirakawa, Ako Kobori. **72 mins.** No rating. Beta, VHS **($59.95);** Laser **($34.95);** CED **($29.95).** Vestron. ★★½

An early attempt by Honda to follow the tremendous success of *Godzilla* tells the story of a prehistoric egg that hatches twin pterodactyls. The film is better directed than most of its kind, though it has its share of silly moments, especially when the big birds are called upon to waddle through the requisite building-stomping scenes. The film's odd shape and short length are due to the deletion of nearly 30 minutes for its American release.

ROLLERBALL (1975) C. *Dir.:* Norman Jewison. *With:* James
Caan, John Beck, John Houseman. **123 mins.** Rated R. Beta, VHS
($69.95); CED **($19.98).** CBS/Fox. ★★

Caan is the "too popular" champion of the violent sport Rollerball, an outlet for the primal emotions of a 21st century society
for which individual violence has been outlawed. The promising
idea of depicting the nature and pressures of professional sports
in the future (taken from Harry Harrison's story "Rollerball Murder") is both overdone and not taken far enough, with Caan's
battle-scarred character becoming an absurd martyr in a plot
about the politics behind the game. The actual games themselves
are impressively designed and ornamented with excellent stunt
work.

SATAN'S SATELLITES (1958) B/W. *Dir.:* Fred C. Brannon. *With:*
Judd Holdren, Aline Towne, Leonard Nimoy. **70 mins.** No rating.
Beta, VHS **($39.95).** Admit One. ★½

See ZOMBIES OF THE STRATOSPHERE.

Rollerball

Saturn 3

SATURN 3 (1980) C. *Dir.:* Stanley Donen. *With:* Kirk Douglas,
Farrah Fawcett, Harvey Keitel. **88 mins.** Rated R. Beta, VHS
($59.98); Laser **($34.98);** CED **($19.98).** CBS/Fox. ★½

Douglas and Fawcett enjoy an idyllic existence in their hy-
droponic garden starship until they are joined by the psychopathic
Keitel and his equally neurotic robot, Hector. What follows is a
ridiculous sort of SF interpretation of the myth of the Serpent's
disruption of Eden, with a seminude Farrah being chased by the
entire male (and mechanical) cast through a dazzling array of
Stuart Craig sets.

SCANNERS (1981) C. *Dir.:* David Cronenberg. *With:* Patrick McGoohan, Stephen Lack, Jennifer O'Neill, Michael Ironside. **102 mins.** Rated R. Beta. VHS **($59.95);** Laser **($34.95);** CED **($29.95).** Embassy. ★★½

Psychic derelict Lack is abducted by a secret telepathic society and learns that his own powers as a "scanner" are second only to those of Ironside, the head of the opposing group. This popular SF-fantasy film is a colorful action piece that begins with the now-classic exploding head scene and builds to an equally bloody psychic war between the two leads. Director Cronenberg achieved widespread attention with this film, his simplest and most commercial, and an ideal place to start any examination of his work.

7TH VOYAGE OF SINBAD, THE (1958) C. *Dir.:* Nathan Hertz (Juran). *With:* Kerwin Mathews, Kathryn Grant, Torin Thatcher. **87 mins.** Rated G. Beta, VHS **($69.95);** CED **($19.95).** RCA/Columbia. ★★★½

The first of Ray Harryhausen's Sinbad features is still the best. Valiant Mathews battles indomitable monsters that guard the path to an egg demanded by magician Thatcher as ransom for an abducted princess. Among the many wonders are a terrifying Cyclops, a two-headed bird, a serpent-woman, and a sword-wielding skeleton (an idea taken much further in the subsequent *Jason and the Argonauts*), all brought to life as much by Bernard Herrmann's score as by Harryhausen's ingenious modeling.

SHADOWMAN (1973) C. *Dir.:* Georges Franju. *With:* Gert Frobe, Gayle Hunnicutt, Jacques Champreux. **88 mins.** Rated PG. Beta, VHS **($39.95).** Cult. ★★½

This lyrical French fantasy follows the exploits of a crimson-hooded, master criminal and his beautiful, masked accomplice as they stoop to conquer an ancient order of Templar Knights and an army of the walking dead in order to attain an ancient treasure. In this budget-conscious production, only Hunnicutt's cat walk across Parisian rooftops conveys Franju's usual haunting brilliance. The film was unavoidably bruised after its condensation from *L'Homme sans visage*, a 400-minute French miniseries.

SHAGGY DOG, THE (1959) B/W. *Dir.:* Charles Barton. *With:* Fred MacMurray, Tommy Kirk, Annette Funicello. **104 mins.** Rated G. Beta, VHS **($69.95);** Laser **($34.95);** CED **($19.98).** Disney. ★★½

Mailman's son Kirk obtains a magical scarab ring that transforms him into a sheepdog whenever, for comedy's sake, it's least convenient. This freewheeling fantasy-comedy is good clean fun, featuring a wonderfully familiar supporting cast (Cecil Kellaway, Strother Martin, Jack Albertson) and a rousing defeat for a bunch of sinister baddies. The transformation effects are played for laughs and good enough to get them.

SHOUT, THE (1979) C. *Dir.:* Jerry Skolimowski. *With:* Alan Bates, Susannah York, John Hurt. **87 mins.** Rated R. Beta, VHS **($59.95);** CED **($29.95).** RCA/Columbia. ★★★

A fascinating Robert Graves tale about Bates, a student of aboriginal magic, who uses his sorcerous knowledge to disrupt the household and marriage of composer Hurt and wife York. Like *Them!,* this is a picture that disorients and intimidates primarily through sound, yet constantly allures with an uncommon intricacy of woven images. Skolimowski finally achieved wide recognition for being the fine artist he is with his next production, *Moonlighting.*

SILENT RUNNING (1971) C. *Dir.:* Douglas Trumbull. *With:* Bruce Dern, Cliff Potts, Jesse Vint. **89 mins.** Rated G. Beta, VHS **($59.95).** MCA. ★★½

The spaceship Valley Forge contains the last of Earth's hydroponically preserved plantlife, lovingly cared for by space ranger Dern, who goes berserk when orders are received to destroy the cargo. After a decade of playing raucous psychotics in supporting roles, Dern was cast here as the sensitive lead; the result is more or less the same role he'd been playing all those years, except it's a lead role and his insanity is supposedly forgivable because it is pro-ecology! Trumbull's direction is intermittently lovely and gentle, highlighting some excellent special effects, but he must regret drowning out his own poignancy with the syrup of Joan Baez ballads.

SIMON (1980) C. *Dir.:* Marshall Brickman. *With:* Alan Arkin, Madeline Kahn, William Finley. **97 mins.** Rated PG. Beta, VHS **($59.95).** Warner. ★★

Brickman, heretofore Woody Allen's screenwriting collaborator, broke out on his own with this mild SF-fantasy about scientist Arkin's peculiarities being misinterpreted by his colleagues as indications of an alien intelligence. Quite a disappointment, considering Brickman's reputation and a seemingly invulnerable cast (Finley, Fred Gwynne, Austin Pendleton—they should talk about Arkin's peculiarities!), with Arkin's pantomime of man's evolution an all too brief highlight.

SINBAD AND THE EYE OF THE TIGER (1977) C. *Dir.:* Sam Wanamaker. *With:* Patrick Wayne, Jane Seymour, Taryn Power. **113 mins.** Rated G. Beta, VHS **($69.95);** Laser **($29.95);** CED **($19.98).** RCA/Columbia. ★★

Ray Harryhausen's follow-up to his box-office success *The Golden Voyage of Sinbad* (see review) is a lackluster production with its "marvels" all minor rethinkings of earlier creations—the troglodyte is *7th Voyage*'s Cyclops, the insect-djinns are like *Jason*'s skeleton legions, and the giant walrus is much like the enormous tortoise in *One Million Years B.C..* The baboon is wonderful, but overall the effects are darker and grainier than they should be.

SINBAD THE SAILOR (1947) C. *Dir.:* Richard Wallace. *With:* Douglas Fairbanks, Jr., Maureen O'Hara, Anthony Quinn, Walter Slezak. **117 mins.** No rating. Beta, VHS **($19.95).** Nostalgia Merchant. ★★★

Fairbanks is quite dashing in a role worthy of his family name as he pursues Arabian princess O'Hara (casting you couldn't get away with today!) and a magical amulet to the ends of the earth. Very good as an actioner or as an Arabian Nights piece of exotica, but its fantasy elements are minor and rather flimsy.

Silent Running

Slapstick of Another Kind

SLAPSTICK OF ANOTHER KIND (1984) C. *Dir.:* Steven Paul. *With:* Jerry Lewis, Madeline Kahn, Marty Feldman, Pat Morita. **82 mins.** Rated PG. Beta, VHS **($79.95);** Laser **($34.95).** Vestron. ★★

Superintelligent twins Wilbur and Eliza (Lewis and Kahn) are shunned by their celebrity parents (also Lewis and Kahn), who don't realize that they are actually aliens capable of saving Earth from itself—but the children become moronic when separated and lose sight of their purpose. An okay film, saved by energetic lunacy from Lewis, but a wretched adaptation of Kurt Vonnegut's novel that can only be attributed to the inexperience of a very young director (Paul was in his early 20s).

SLAUGHTERHOUSE FIVE (1972) C. *Dir.:* George Roy Hill. *With:* Michael Sacks, Ron Liebman, Eugene Roche, Valerie Perrine. **104 mins.** Rated R. Beta, VHS **($39.95).** MCA. ★★★½

This film version of Vonnegut's novel tells the epiphanic tale of Billy Pilgrim, who's become "unstuck in time" and jolts abruptly, backwards and forwards, between the decades of his long life—from his amusing but sad childhood to the time he spent in WWII Dresden, from his wife's hilarious death to his abduction by aliens (who mate him with starlet Montana Wildhack on the planet Tralfamadore). The film introduced Perrine and Perry King, but Liebman is overwhelming as Billy's lifelong enemy. An exquisite and unusual look at a good and full life.

SLEEPER (1973) C. *Dir.:* Woody Allen. *With:* Woody Allen, Diane Keaton, John Beck. **88 mins.** Rated PG. Beta, VHS **($59.98);** Laser **($34.98);** CED **($19.98).** CBS/Fox. ★★★½

Allen is the proprietor of a 1970s health food store, who is awakened from a deep freeze 200 years in the future, after cigarettes and candy have been proven beneficial and yogurt and beansprouts lethal. His hilarious misadventures include masquerading as a robot servant, discovering a giant garden (he slips on a giant banana peel!), and joining an underground revolution. Allen's most even and funniest movie.

SOME CALL IT LOVING (1973) C. *Dir.:* James B. Harris. *With:* Zalman King, Tisa Farrow, Carol White. **103 mins.** Rated R. Beta, VHS **($59.95).** Monterey. ★★★

The indolently wealthy King buys "Sleeping Beauty" Farrow from a carnival sideshow, awakens her with a kiss, and involves her in a series of staged erotic fantasies. Loosely based on a John Collier short story, this isn't a sex film but rather a sentimentally romantic fantasy about how reality often falls short of what we imagine. Never given adequate theatrical release but well worth seeing, not least of all for an early (and surprisingly touching) cameo by Richard Pryor.

Slaughterhouse Five   Somewhere in Time

SOMEWHERE IN TIME (1980) C. *Dir.:* Jeannot Szwarc. *With:* Christopher Reeve, Jane Seymour, Christopher Plummer **103 mins.** Rated PG. Beta, VHS **($79.95)**; Laser **($29.98)**. MCA. ★★★½

Playwright Reeve becomes obsessed with a photograph of turn-of-the-century actress Seymour and mentally "suggests" himself backwards through time, where they meet, fall in love, and solve a mystery about his own future life. This film is as romantic as movies come, and fortunately lacks the directorial manipulations that all too frequently cheat audiences. Director Szwarc's only sincere film, adapted by Richard Matheson from his novel *Bid Time Return,* is well acted by all.

SON OF BLOB (1972) C. *Dir.:* Larry Hagman. *With:* Robert Walker, Jr., Godfrey Cambridge, Carol Lynley. **87 mins.** Rated PG. Beta, VHS **($59.95)**. Video Gems. ★★

This sequel to 1958's *The Blob* (see review) was a very long time in coming, and the result is a fairly amusing, if never frightening, wallow in weird nostalgia. Cambridge accidentally thaws the Blob from its icy resting place, unleashing it on a film teeming with "guest stars" like Shelley Berman, Burgess Meredith, and director Hagman himself. Ironically, it's *this* part of this uneven film that works, not the main plot about small-town authority figures who ignore the warnings of responsible teens.

SON OF FLUBBER (1962) B/W. *Dir.:* Robert Stevenson. *With:* Fred MacMurray, Nancy Olson, Tommy Kirk. **100 mins.** Rated G. Beta, VHS **($69.95).** Disney. ★★½

This sequel to *The Absent-Minded Professor* stretches the notion of "flubber" to absurd lengths, with college prof MacMurray now dabbling in weather control and souped-up football games. Hasn't much of the original film's sense of wonder, but a mini-documentary insert about the commercializing of flubber is a hilarious satire of the advertising industry.

SON OF GODZILLA (1969) C. *Dir.:* Jun Fukuda. *With:* Tadao Takashima, Akira Kubo, Kenji Sahara. **86 mins.** No rating. Beta, VHS **($44.95).** Budget. ★½

This film introduces Minya, the gnomic offspring of everyone's favorite Tokyo stomper-*cum*-savior Godzilla, who blows stunning smoke rings at assorted giant bugs. The series had been on the downslope for many years but, after the death of Inoshiro Honda, the Toho studios took the Godzilla character to amazing depths of self-parody.

SON OF KONG (1933) B/W. *Dir.:* Ernest B. Schoedsack. *With:* Robert Armstrong, Helen Mack, Frank Reicher. **70 mins.** No rating. Beta, VHS **($N/A).** Nostalgia Merchant. ★★½

Whimsical *King Kong* sequel has the conscience-stricken Armstrong returning to Skull Island and finding Kong's cute albino offspring. Short and inoffensive, it was rushed to theaters before the year of *Kong's* own release expired. As always, Willis O'Brien's stop-motion animation is as endearing as it is groundbreaking.

SON OF SINBAD (1955) C. *Dir.:* Ted Tetzlaff. *With:* Dale Robertson, Vincent Price, Mari Blanchard. **88 mins.** No rating. Beta, VHS **($54.95).** VCI. ★★

Robertson, of all people, is the favorite son of the Arabian Nights in this modest, unassuming grade-B programmer. He is trapped by an evil caliph (Price, of course, in a better piece of casting) and told to obtain the secret of Greek fire in order to liberate his city. Bland exotica.

SORCERESS (1982) C. *Dir.:* Brian Stuart. *With:* Leigh & Lynette Harris, Robert Ballesteros, Martin LaSalle. **83 mins.** Rated PG. Beta, VHS **($69.95).** Thorn EMI. ★½

Young female twins are educated in sorcery and sword crossing by a benevolent wizard so that they may defeat their father Triagon, a Master of Darkness who nearly sacrificed them in their infancy for satanic favor. The script (by Jim Wynorski) doesn't give director or cast much to work with. This low-budget fantasy is poorly made and acted, with surprisingly little nudity for a New World Picture.

Sorceress

Soylent Green

SOYLENT GREEN (1973) C. *Dir.:* Richard Fleischer. *With:* Charlton Heston, Edward G. Robinson, Leigh Taylor-Young. **97 mins.** Rated PG. Beta, VHS **($59.95);** Laser **($34.95);** CED **($29.95).** MGM/UA. ★★

More of the overbearing, socially righteous, mealymouthed SF in which Heston briefly specialized. In the 21st century, overpopulation has become so out of hand that citizens must turn themselves into literal "retirement" centers, and the living are sustained by a form of sanitized cannibalism. Robinson is poignant in his final performance as a man old enough to remember the tastes and smells of real life, and Heston is well entrenched in his jaw-jutting self-parody.

SPACE PATROL 1 (1955) B/W. *Dir.:* Dik Darley. *With:* Ed Kemmer, Lyn Osborne, Ken Mayer. **120 mins.** No rating. Beta, VHS **($N/A).** Nostalgia Merchant. ★½

These kinescopes of the popular 1950s SF teleseries chronicle the adventures of Space Patrol, Commander in Chief Buzz Corey, and his bone-headed aide, Cadet Happy, as they battle the enemies of the United Planets. Cheaply produced for live television and imbued with a comic condescension for its subject matter, it is otherwise not too dissimilar from the much later *Star Trek* series. Best suited for those who remember the original broadcasts.

SPACE PATROL 2 (1955) B/W. *Dir.:* Dik Darley. *With:* Ed Kemmer, Lyn Osborne, Ken Mayer. **120 mins.** No rating. Beta, VHS **(SN/A).** Nostalgia Merchant. ★½
   More of the same. See SPACE PATROL 1.

SPACE RAIDERS (1981) C. *Dir.:* Howard R. Cohen. *With:* Vince Edwards, David Mendenhall, Thom Christopher, Dick Miller. **84 mins.** Rated PG. Beta, VHS **($39.98).** Warner. ★★
   The first movie Roger Corman produced after his departure from New World is a disappointment about a 10-year-old boy's space adventures amongst monsters, mercenaries, and just plain characters. Famed character actor Dick Miller illuminates this weak production briefly as a used spaceship dealer. Otherwise a naked excuse for reusing stock footage.

SPACED OUT (1981) C. *Dir.:* Norman J. Warren. *With:* Barry Stokes, Glory Annen, Lynne Ross. **84 mins.** Rated R. Beta, VHS **($59.95).** VidAmerica. ★
   Sexy aliens abduct Earth men and use them to learn about terrestrial forms of lovemaking. Naughty SF-comedy is a senseless reworking of a theme done much more enjoyably in the fifties, when they couldn't show anything.

SPACEHUNTER: ADVENTURES IN THE FORBIDDEN ZONE (1983) C. *Dir.:* Lamont Johnson. *With:* Peter Strauss, Molly Ringwald, Michael Ironside. **90 mins.** Rated PG. Beta Hi-Fi, VHS **($79.95);** Laser **($29.95);** CED **($19.98).** RCA/Columbia ★½
   Strauss is a galactic adventurer who, with "help" from brat Ringwald, challenges the evil man-machine Overdog (Ironside, proving he can be good in anything) for the release of three female prisoners. Nothing plot gets no help from modest-scale special effects in this weary, commercial-minded jump on the SF bandwagon. Originally shown in dark, unwatchable 3-D, the film is unwatchable without it, too.

SPACESHIP (1983) C. *Dir.:* Bruce Kimmel. *With:* Leslie Nielsen, Cindy Williams, Patrick Macnee. **80 mins.** Rated PG. Beta, VHS **($69.95).** Vestron. ★

A painfully lame attempt at a musical parody of *Alien,* as a space crew discovers a stowaway monster who likes to sing and dance. The quality cast is debased and degraded by endless, idiotic groaner material. Originally titled *The Creature Wasn't Nice* and never released to theaters (it's a cinch to see why).

Spacehunter

Spy Smasher

SPY SMASHER (1942) B/W. *Dir.:* William Witney. *With:* Kane Richman, Sam Flint, Marguerite Chapman. **185 mins.** No rating. Beta, VHS **($79.95).** Republic. ★★★

An exciting 12-episode serial from Republic Studios starring Spy Smasher, a costumed advocate of the American Way born in the pages of *Whiz Comics.* His enemy is The Mask, the leader of a Nazi spy ring against whom our hero employs ray guns, a "batplane" (wasn't that someone else's idea?), and some terrific derring-do. Director Witney was the finest director of Hollywood serials (see *The Adventures of Captain Marvel*) and his touch is more than evident here.

STARCRASH (1979) C. *Dir.:* Lewis Coates (Luigi Cozzi). *With:* Caroline Munro, Marjoe Gortner, Christopher Plummer. **92 mins.** Rated PG. Beta, VHS **($69.95);** Laser. Embassy. ★★

Space hoodlum Zarth Arn (Spinell) has delusions of grandeur, and wants the whole galaxy under his thumb—starting with adventuress Stella Star. A very bad movie that's very easy to like; it's hard to feel contempt for something so self-consciously hokey. Made in Italy, it's also one of the few films to make prominent use of cult actress Munro, looking smashing in low-cut leather costumes.

STARMAN (1984) C. *Dir.:* John Carpenter. *With:* Jeff Bridges, Karen Allen, Charles Martin Smith. **115 mins.** Rated PG. Beta Hi-Fi, VHS Hi-Fi **($79.95).** RCA/Columbia. ⧠® ★★★
    A curious alien responds to the Voyager spacecraft's invitation to visit Earth. He assumes the form of Allen's dead husband and journeys cross country with her to the rendezvous point for his return voyage. While en route, he learns much about the pleasures and the ironies of human existence, and becomes involved in an inevitable romance while trying to evade the maneuvers of our heartless government, which wants to capture the alien and dissect him. Although thoroughly predictable, the film is nonetheless satisfying. Bridges was Oscar-nominated for a role that relies on stiff mimicry, but Allen's touching vulnerability shines through.

STAR TREK: A TASTE OF ARMAGEDDON (1967) C. *Dir.:* Joseph Pevney. *With:* Series cast (William Shatner, Leonard Nimoy, De-Forest Kelley, James Doohan, George Takei, Nichelle Nichols), Barbara Babcock, David Opatoshu. **51 mins.** No rating. Beta, VHS **($14.95).** Paramount. ★★
    Another Kirk vs. computer saga pits the Enterprise commander against the centuries-old system of computerized war which tabulates victims who must then report to disintegration chambers. Too verbal to be very gripping, this episode has Enterprise crew openly fulfilling their duty as ambassadors for the human side of science fiction.

STAR TREK: AMOK TIME (1967) C. *Dir.:* Joseph Pevney. *With:* Series cast, Celia Lovsky, Arlene Martel. **51 mins.** No rating. Beta, VHS **($14.95).** Paramount. ★★★
    Fits of unusual irritability lead the Enterprise crew to discover that their traditionally cool Mr. Spock is nearing his native mating season. An unscheduled expedition to Vulcan leads to a death duel between Spock and his betrothed's chosen champion, Captain Kirk. Written by SF novelist Theodore Sturgeon, it is one of the series' better episodes, with some nice surprises.

STAR TREK: ARENA (1967) C. *Dir.:* Joseph Pevney. *With:* Series cast, Carole Shelyne, Vic Perrin. **51 mins.** No rating. Beta, VHS **($14.95).** Paramount. ★★½
    Based on a non-SF story by Frederic Brown, the episode begins as the Enterprise's high-speed pursuit of a Goran ship is

interrupted by members of a superior race who plant the two captains on small asteroid with instructions to settle their disagreements there. Poor makeup doesn't detract too much from an otherwise enjoyable, action-oriented episode.

STAR TREK: BALANCE OF TERROR (1966) C. *Dir.:* Vincent McEveety. *With:* Series cast, Mark Lenard, John Warburton. **51 mins.** No rating. Beta, VHS **($14.95).** Paramount. ★★½
  A delicate situation is well milked for drama and suspense as a Romulan ship tests Earth's defenses 100 years after a devastating war between the two races. The episode is best remembered for introducing diabolical Romulans and Neutral Zones to the series. Lenard was eventually to play all three of *Star Trek*'s resident aliens: Klingons, Romulans, *and* Vulcans (as Spock's father!).

STAR TREK: CHARLIE X (1966) C. *Dir.:* Lawrence Dobkin. *With:* Series cast, Robert Walker, Jr., Abraham Sofaer. **51 mins.** No rating. Beta, VHS **($14.95).** Paramount. ★★★
  The Enterprise rescues a teenage survivor of an ill-fated space expedition, and the crew slowly grows aware that he is possessed of unwholesome, extra-human abilities. An interesting episode, one that conjures a more realistic portrait of evil than usual. Quite satisfying.

Mr. Spock

Chief Engineer Scottie

STAR TREK: CITY ON THE EDGE OF FOREVER (1967) C. *Dir.:* Gene Roddenberry. *With:* Series cast, Joan Collins, David L. Ross. **51 mins.** No rating. Beta, VHS **($14.95).** Paramount. ★★★½
  This eloquent, poetic episode (written by SF great Harlan Elli-

son) details the fundamental problems of trying to change time. Kirk is accidentally swept back to 1930s New York, where he falls into a bittersweet relationship with Collins. A rare instance of televised science fiction approaching the standards of emotion and complexity which exist in the best science fiction literature.

STAR TREK: CONSCIENCE OF THE KING (1966) C. *Dir.:* Gerd Oswald. *With:* Series cast, Arnold Moss, Barbara Anderson. **51 mins.** No rating. Beta, VHS **($14.95).** Paramount. ★★½

The Enterprise picks up a crew of Shakespearean actors whose leader may or may not be the murderous dictator (long presumed dead) responsible for the deaths of Kirk's family. The episode has some tense moments, but is surprisingly carried more by Elizabethan hyperbole and Oswald's directorial flair than high action. Works well despite its talky bent.

STAR TREK: COURT-MARTIAL (1967) C. *Dir.:* Marc Daniels. *With:* Series cast, Elisha Cook, Jr., Alice Rawlings. **51 mins.** No rating. Beta, VHS **($14.95).** Paramount. ★★

Kirk's opinion on the cause of a crewman's death is contested by the Enterprise's computer, resulting in a shocking court-martial trial (in which he is defended by Cook, the most suspicious-looking actor who's ever lived). Despite the arresting nature of the plot, the episode pans out as merely average, due to a cop-out finale that one sees coming from a mile away.

STAR TREK: DAGGER OF THE MIND (1966) C. *Dir.:* Vincent McEveety. *With:* Series cast, James Gregory, Morgan Woodward. **51 mins.** No rating. Beta, VHS **($14.95).** Paramount. ★★½

Kirk investigates the cruelties at a penal colony and discovers the use of a sadistic throne. The episode includes the first presentation of Vulcan mind-melding, through which a shocking revelation is made. The episode has good atmosphere and an anti-technological message.

STAR TREK: DEVIL IN THE DARK (1967) C. *Dir.:* Joseph Pevney. *With:* Series cast, Ken Lynch, Janos Prohaska. **51 mins.** No rating. Beta, VHS **($14.95).** Paramount. ★★★

A silicon-based, rock-tunneling creature, the last of its race, is killing miners who threaten its nest of eggs. Spock mind-melds to negotiate an agreement between the two species. Scary moments build to intellectually satisfying settlement.

STAR TREK: ERRAND OF MERCY (1967) C. *Dir.:* John Newland. *With:* Series cast, John Colicos, John Abbott. **51 mins.** No rating. Beta, VHS **($14.95).** Paramount. ★★★

Colicos plays the Klingon leader in the series' introduction of this race. The Enterprise intervenes on behalf of targeted pacifist planet against Klingon attack. Good action and delightfully unexpected conclusion make this one of the series' finest hours.

STAR TREK: JOURNEY TO BABEL (1967) C. *Dir.:* Joseph Pevney. *With:* Series cast, Jane Wyatt, Mark Lenard, Reggie Nalder. **51 mins.** No rating. Beta, VHS **($14.95).** Paramount. ★★½

Spock's parents are introduced in this slightly above average episode, in which Kirk must navigate stormy diplomatic waters while transporting a cadre of intergalactic ambassadors to a much-needed peace conference.

STAR TREK: LET THAT BE YOUR LAST BATTLEFIELD (1969) C. *Dir.:* Jud Taylor. *With:* Series cast, Frank Gorshin, Lou Antonio. **51 mins.** No rating. Beta, VHS **($14.95).** Paramount. ★½

The Enterprise intercepts a stolen shuttlecraft containing Gorshin, a representative of a bizarre half-black, half-white race that cannot peaceably coexist with itself. Heavy-handed treatment of then contemporary racial issues firmly root this futuristic drama in the best forgotten confusions of the past. Otherwise notable for Kirk's only command (until *Star Trek III: The Search for Spock*) to destroy the Enterprise.

STAR TREK: MIRI (1966) C. *Dir.:* Vincent McEveety. *With:* Series cast, Kim Darby, Michael J. Pollard. **51 mins.** No rating. Beta, VHS **($14.95).** Paramount. ★★½

The Enterprise explores a planet where an ancient expedition conducted immortality experiments, killing off all adults and leaving behind a populace of 300-year-old, virus-infected children just beginning to enter puberty. A search for an antidote keeps events perking along. Not bad, about par for the excellent first season.

STAR TREK: MIRROR, MIRROR (1967) C. *Dir.:* Marc Daniels. *With:* Series cast, Vic Perrin, Barbara Luna. **51 mins.** No rating. Beta, VHS **($14.95).** Paramount. ★★½

This second season episode begins as an ion storm sweeps the Enterprise officers into a parallel universe, where they find themselves occupying an Enterprise where assassination is the common means of advancement. Their struggle to return through a space window before it recloses provides neat against-the-clock anxiety. An above average episode from the second season.

STAR TREK: MUDD'S WOMEN (1966) C. *Dir.:* Harvey Hart. *With:* Series cast, Roger C. Carmel, Karen Steele. **51 mins.** No rating. Beta, VHS **($14.95).** Paramount. ★★
    Robert Bloch's script introduces the recurring adversary Carmel who, in this episode, is shipping "enhanced" beauties to lonely men in deep space. The Enterprise intervenes out of moral indignation. This passable episode has the assured atmosphere of early *Star Trek* episodes, but too much Carmel gums up the works.

STAR TREK: OPERATION ANNIHILATE (1967) C. *Dir.:* Herschell Daugherty. *With:* Series cast, Joan Swift, Maurishka. **51 mins.** No rating. Beta, VHS **($14.95).** Paramount. ★½
    Kirk's visit to his brother at a research outpost uncovers a plague of bat-like aliens threatening to infest the galaxy. A below average episode, hindered by cheap shopping mall sets and an absurdly overstated (hence apathetic) premise and a pat resolution.

Sulu

Uhura

STAR TREK: RETURN OF THE ARCHONS (1967) C. *Dir.:* Joseph Pevney. *With:* Series cast, Perry Townes, John Lormer. **51 mins.** No rating. Beta, VHS **($14.95).** Paramount. ★★
    This technology-is-evil parable has the Enterprise discovering a rural agrarian society dominated by a concealed computer. A description that fits several other episodes in the series; Kirk sorts out the problem here with a minimum of fuss.

STAR TREK: THE ALTERNATIVE FACTOR (1967) C. *Dir.:* Gerd Oswald. *With:* Robert Brown, Richard Darr. **51 mins.** No rating. Beta, VHS **($14.95).** Paramount. ★½

Muddled nonsense about the Enterprise's attempt to keep an antimatter derelict separated from his positively charged counterpart, a reunion which could potentially discharge the entire universe. A solution to the problem arrives inexplicably, without overconcern for dramatic smoothness. It was perhaps the worst episode as of its original airdate.

STAR TREK: THE CHANGELING (1966) C. *Dir.:* Marc Daniels. *With:* Series cast, Vic Perrin, Barbara Gates. **51 mins.** No rating. Beta, VHS **($14.95).** CED **($19.98).** Paramount. ★★★

An episode notable as the basis for the first *Star Trek* feature, in which the Enterprise meets a 200-year-old space probe from Earth which, following alien collision, has expanded its powers and purpose, destroying anything that doesn't stack up to its computer-like criteria.

STAR TREK: THE CORBOMITE MANEUVER (1966) C. *Dir.:* Joseph Sargent. *With:* Series cast, Clint Howard, Anthony Call. **51 mins.** No rating. Beta, VHS **($14.95).** Paramount. ★★★

The Enterprise is threatened by an energy-consuming space entity, a free-floating cornucopia whose open vacuum end is drawing them ever inward. Unusually crisp direction by Sargent *(Colossus: The Forbin Project)*, with the cast still riding high from first season adrenaline. The resolution is something of a letdown.

STAR TREK: THE ENEMY WITHIN (1966) C. *Dir.:* Leo Penn. *With:* Series cast, Jim Goodwin, Garland Thompson. **51 mins.** No rating. Beta, VHS **($14.95).** Paramount. ★★★

Trouble in the transporter room splits Captain Kirk into two Kirks—one possessed of his good traits, the other of his evil ones. The well-conceived Richard Matheson script isolates the interesting truth that the good Kirk is unable to command the ship—that a touch of egoism and cruelty is necessary to run a taut Enterprise. So clever that Shatner's operatic overacting in the evil role is completely forgivable.

STAR TREK: THE GALILEO SEVEN (1967) C. *Dir.:* Robert Gist. *With:* Series cast, Don Marshall, Rees Vaughn. **51 mins.** No rating. Beta, VHS **($14.95).** Paramount. ★★★

Episode centers on Spock's first shot at command on a shuttlecraft mission with the shuttlecraft stalled on a treacherous, monster-laden planet. The Vulcan's logical mind becomes the core of the narrative as he tries to oust his charges from the dilemma at hand. Fine dramatic and action situations with enjoyably anxious finale.

STAR TREK: THE MAN TRAP (1966) C. *Dir.:* Marc Daniels. *With:* Series cast, Jeanne Bal, Alfred Ryder. **51 mins.** No rating. Beta, VHS **($14.95).** Paramount. ★★

This episode tells the story of a creature beamed aboard that adapts appearance of trusted persons to vampirize the Enterprise crew for their biological salt. A serviceable but undistinguished episode, written by George Clayton Johnson *(Logan's Run)* and occasionally enlivened by Fred Phillips' monster design.

STAR TREK: THE MENAGERIE (1966) C. *Dir.:* Marc Daniels and Robert Butler. *With:* Series cast, Jeffrey Hunter, Susan Oliver. **100 mins.** No rating. Beta, VHS **($14.95).** Paramount. ★★★

The series' only two-parter is rewardingly thoughtful and thorough, as Spock is court-martialed for abduction of the Enterprise and its former captain. Of special interest, the episode incorporates entirety of *The Cage,* the original never-aired pilot featuring Jeffrey Hunter in the lead.

STAR TREK: THE NAKED TIME (1966) C. *Dir.:* Marc Daniels. *With:* Series cast, Bruce Hyde, Stewart Moss. **51 mins.** No rating. Beta, VHS **($14.95).** Paramount. ★★

A virus infects the Enterprise causing the crew to go insane. One of those endlessly enjoyable episodes which allow Spock's suppressed emotions to shine through his Vulcan surface. Each of the series regulars is given center stage to interpret the effects of the fever on their personalities; the episode delivers what is expected, no more and no less.

STAR TREK: THE SQUIRE OF GOTHOS (1967) C. *Dir.:* Donald McDougall. *With:* Series cast, William Campbell, Venita Wolf. **51 mins.** No rating. Beta, VHS **($14.95).** Paramount. ★★

An all-powerful alien uses the Enterprise officers as playthings until his parents intervene at the hour's end. A watchable but wishy-washy treatment of hoary SF concept, already done to death on *The Twilight Zone* and other programs. This, the first of several uses of this theme in the series, was also the most satisfactory.

STAR TREK: THE THOLIAN WEB (1968) C. *Dir.:* Ralph Senensky. *With:* Series cast. **51 mins.** No rating. Beta, VHS **($55.95)**, CED **($19.98).** Paramount. ★★

One of the few episodes from the third season to rank this high. After Kirk disappears into deep space, the crew stumbles about to regain an authority figure. Meanwhile, aliens announce the ship is trespassing and ensnare it in an invisible web. This fair episode boasts an interesting use of special effects.

STAR TREK: THE TROUBLE WITH TRIBBLES (1968) C. *Dir.:* Joseph Pevney. *With:* Series cast, William Schallert, Whit Bissell. **51 mins.** No rating. Beta, VHS **($55.95);** CED **($19.98).** Paramount. ★★★

One of the series' most famous episodes, a lighthearted farce that observes the Enterprise at the mercy of furiously multiplying tiny puff-puffs called tribbles. Kirk's pomposity and Spock's unflinching reactions are perfect foils to the comic (and, make no mistake, *nightmarish*) situation. Good use of familiar supporting actors.

STAR TREK: THIS SIDE OF PARADISE (1967) C. *Dir.:* Ralph Senensky. *With:* Series cast, Jill Ireland, Frank Overton. **51 mins.** No rating. Beta, VHS **($14.95).** Paramount. ★★½

An early antidrug message set on a rural planet where workers are sensually enslaved by the smokey emissions from their leafy harvests. The Enterprise crew catches wind of their situation, so to speak, with Kirk remaining the only voice of reason. Campy and amusing when seen today, with Spock's reactions to spore sniffing a particularly silly sight.

STAR TREK: TOMORROW IS YESTERDAY (1967) C. *Dir.:* Michael O'Herlihy. *With:* Series cast, Roger Perry, Ed Peck. **51 mins.** No rating. Beta, VHS **($14.95).** Paramount. ★★½

The Enterprise is catapulted back in time to Earth in the 1960s and accidentally destroys a fighter aircraft beaming the pilot aboard and becoming embroiled in the problem of restoring the upset balance of time. First series use of well-worn time travel situation; distinguished by commendably fresh handling of material.

STAR TREK: WHAT ARE LITTLE GIRLS MADE OF? (1966) C. *Dir.:* James Goldstone. *With:* Series cast, Michael Strong, Ted Cassidy. **51 mins.** No rating. Beta, VHS **($14.95)**. Paramount. ★★½

A distress signal leads the Enterprise to the rediscovery of a long-lost scientist, the former love of Nurse Chapell (Magel Barrett Roddenberry, a series regular). The crew uncovers his scheme to repopulate the galaxy with androids. The Robert Bloch script plays with more originality than it sounds.

STAR TREK: WHERE NO MAN HAS GONE BEFORE (1966) C. *Dir.:* James Goldstone. *With:* Series cast, Gary Lockwood, Sally Kellerman. **51 mins.** No rating. Beta, VHS **($14.95)**. Paramount. ★★★

The series' second pilot, the first with a famous cast, has the Enterprise bombarded by a mysterious energy which evolves two crew members into god-like beings. This solid, well-written episode features excellent performances and represents an advancement in maturity for televised science fiction. It's fascinating to see Shatner and Nimoy getting their first footholds on their characters.

Star Trek

STAR TREK TV SERIES—VOL 1 (1966) C. *Dir.:* Marc Daniels and Robert Butler. *With:* Series cast. **100 mins.** No rating. Beta, VHS **($55.95)**; Laser **($29.95)**; CED **($19.98)**. Paramount. ★★★

Contains "The Menagerie," the series' only two-part episode. See individual review.

STAR TREK TV SERIES—VOL. 2 (1967) C. *Dir.:* Joseph Pevney. *With:* Series cast. **100 mins.** No rating. Beta, VHS **($55.95)**. Paramount. ★★½

Contains "Amok Time" and "Journey to Babel." See individual reviews.

STAR TREK TV SERIES—VOL. 3 (1968) C. *Dir.:* Marc Daniels and Ralph Senensky. *With:* Series cast. **100 mins.** No rating. Beta, VHS **($55.95).** Paramount. ★★★
Contains "Mirror, Mirror" and "The Tholian Web." See individual reviews.

STAR TREK TV SERIES—VOL. 4 (1968) C. *Dir.:* Joseph Pevney and Jud Taylor. *With:* Series cast. **100 mins.** No rating. Beta, VHS **($55.95).** Paramount. ★★★
Contains "The Trouble With Tribbles" and "Let That Be Your Last Battlefield". See individual reviews.

STAR TREK TV SERIES (1966) C. *Dir.:* Vincent McEveety/Gerd Oswald. *With:* Series cast. **100 mins.** No rating. Laser **($29.95).** Paramount. ★★½
Contains "Balance of Terror" and "Conscience of the King." See individual reviews.

STAR TREK TV SERIES (1966) C. *Dir.:* Various. *With:* Series cast. **100 mins.** No rating. Laser **($29.95).** Paramount. ★★★
Contains "The Galileo Seven" and "Shore Leave." See "The Galileo Seven" for review of that episode.

STAR TREK TV SERIES (1967) C. *Dir.:* Joseph Pevney/Donald McDougall. *With:* Series cast. **100 mins.** No rating. Laser **($29.95).** Paramount. ★★/★★½
Contains "Arena" and "The Squire of Gothos." See individual reviews.

STAR TREK TV SERIES (1967) C. *Dir.:* Marc Daniels/Michael O'Herlihy. *With:* Series cast. **100 mins.** No rating. Laser **($29.95).** Paramount. ★★/★★½
Contains "Court Martial" and "Tomorrow Is Yesterday." See individual reviews.

STAR TREK TV SERIES (1967) C. *Dir.:* Various. *With:* Series cast. **100 mins.** No rating. Laser **($29.95).** Paramount. ★★
Contains "Return of the Archons" and "Space Seed." See "Return of the Archons" for review of that episode.

STAR TREK TV II (1968) C. *Dir.:* Gene Roddenberry and Jud Taylor. *With:* Series cast. **100 mins.** No rating. CED **($19.98).** Paramount. ★★★
   A special CED pressing of *Star Trek* double feature, "The City on the Edge of Forever" and "Let That Be Your Last Battlefield." See individual reviews.

STAR TREK TV III (1968) C. *Dir.:* Joseph Pevney and Ralph Senensky. *With:* Series cast. **100 mins.** No rating. CED **($19.98).** Paramount. ★★★
   A special CED pressing of *Star Trek* double feature, "The Trouble With Tribbles" and "The Tholian Web." See individual reviews.

STAR TREK IV (1968) C. *Dir.:* Marc Daniels and Ralph Senensky. *With:* Series cast. **100 mins.** No rating. CED **($19.98).** Paramount. ★★½
   A special CED pressing of *Star Trek* double feature, "Mirror, Mirror" and "The Tholian Web." Yes, "The Tholian Web" *again*. See individual reviews.

STAR TREK: THE MOTION PICTURE (1979) C. *Dir.:* Robert Wise. *With:* William Shatner, Leonard Nimoy, DeForest Kelley, Persis Khambatta. **143 mins.** Rated G. Beta Hi-Fi, VHS **($39.95);** Laser **($39.95);** CED **($34.98).** Paramount. ★★
   The U.S.S. Enterprise arrived on the big screen with this momentous thud, a pompous, overblown variation on two TV episodes, "The Changling" and "The Doomsday Machine." Here, the starship investigates "V'ger," the source of a deadly earthbound emanation. Gorgeous Douglas Trumbull effects are combined with laughably overused shots of awestruck cast (the video release contains an additional 13 minutes not seen in theaters).

STAR TREK II: THE WRATH OF KAHN (1982) C. *Dir.:* Nicholas Meyer. *With:* William Shatner, Leonard Nimoy, Ricardo Montalban. **113 mins.** Rated PG. Beta Hi-Fi, VHS **($39.95);** Laser **($29.95);** CED **($19.98).** Paramount. ★★★½
   This sequel to the 1967 TV episode "Space Seed" (see review) is undoubtedly the high point of the entire *Star Trek* saga, as genetic superman Khan wreaks his vengeance against Kirk and the Enterprise for stranding him for many years on a barren planet. Montalban attacks his role with startling vigor, reminding us that there's a real actor beneath that *Fantasy Island* exterior,

Star Trek II: The Wrath of Khan   Star Wars

and Spock's death scene is the best work Nimoy has done, moving even for nonfanatical viewers. Best of all, director Meyer stresses the narrative value of thematic motifs and weaves them into a pleasingly symphonic statement of life, loss, and adventure.

STAR TREK III: THE SEARCH FOR SPOCK (1984) C. *Dir.:* Leonard Nimoy. *With:* William Shatner, DeForest Kelley, George Takei. **105 mins.** Rated PG. Beta Hi-Fi, VHS Hi-Fi **($29.95);** Laser **($29.95);** CED **($29.95).** Paramount.◻® ★★½

The sequel to *Star Trek II: The Wrath of Khan* opens with Kirk hijacking the antiquated starship Enterprise to attempt a rejuvenation of dead Spock on the planet Genesis. Along the way, the crew must confront the Klingons, who want to steal the planet's secret for use against the Federation. A good people-oriented story, but it is marred by workman-like direction from Nimoy and tacky Klingon makeup.

STAR WARS (1977) C. *Dir.:* George Lucas. *With:* Mark Hamill, Harrison Ford, Carrie Fisher. **121 mins.** Rated PG. Beta, VHS **($39.95);** Laser **($34.98);** CED **($19.98).** CBS/Fox. ★★★★

"A long time ago in a galaxy far, far away," space teen Luke Skywalker buys a pair of servant droids, accidentally triggering from one of them a holographic recording of an abducted princess' distress signal. The message gives his aimless life definition and clarifies the mysteries of his past. It also led to one of the greatest success stories in film history. A thoroughly winning combination of SF, fantasy, and adventure which borrows shamelessly from classic SF serials, but uses these tried-'n'-true elements to forge an unbelievably *new* style of science fiction filmmaking.

STRANGE INVADERS (1983) C. *Dir.:* Michael Laughlin. *With:* Paul LeMat, Nancy Allen, Diana Scarwid. **94 mins.** Rated PG. Beta, VHS **($79.95);** Laser **($34.95);** CED **($19.98).** Vestron. ★★½

A spoof of fifties SF movies about aliens who are insidiously conquering small-town America. It begins with the confidence of a classic, but its tongue grows numb in its cheek and ultimately the storyline is taken too seriously. Worth catching anyway for its superbly composed first half, cameo bits by familiar fifties faces, and grody makeup effects.

STRANGER FROM VENUS (1954) B/W. *Dir.:* Burt Balaban. *With:* Patricia Neal, Helmut Dantine. **78 mins.** No rating. Beta, VHS **($N/A).** Nostalgia Merchant. ★★

Intellectual alien Dantine arrives to warn us of the dangers inherent in our nuclear research. His pacificity arouses suspicion and the arrival of a second flying saucer arouses fear. Uncredited as such, but a virtual remake of classic *The Day the Earth Stood Still* (minus the Earth standing still), with Neal reprising her role as the sympathetic, nonreactionary woman. Interesting, but it doesn't begin to approach the sterling integrity and breathless excitement of the original.

STRYKER (1983) C. *Dir.:* Cirio H. Santiago. *With:* Steve Sandor, Andria Savio, Monique St. Pierre. **84 mins.** Rated R. Beta, VHS **($69.95).** Embassy. ★

An unendurable New World production works from the premise that, following the nuclear apocalypse, water becomes Earth's most precious commodity. When a wandering tribe discovers a fresh spring, a woman initiates an internal conflict by wanting to share it with neighboring colonies, a viewpoint shared only by the hero of the title. This alleged SF action piece is boring and slow, tossing elements of *The Road Warrior, Star Wars,* and *Raiders of the Lost Ark* into a blender with absolutely no art surviving.

SUMMER OF SECRETS (1976) C. *Dir.:* Jim Sharman. *With:* Arthur Dignam, Rufus Collins, Nell Campbell. **100 mins.** Rated R. Beta, VHS **($69.95).** VidAmerica. ★★★

An old scientist hires a director and kidnaps a woman to stage and film his dead wife's memories for orientation purposes after he restores her cryogenically preserved body to life. This Australian-made fantasy takes its time explaining what's going on, but this bizarre cross between *Pygmalion* and *The Bride of Frankenstein* holds one's interest even at low ebb. Sharman, who also directed *The Rocky Horror Picture Show,* imbues the film with haunting images, art deco furnishings, and a visible contortion of pain resting just below its prettiness.

SUPER FUZZ (1981) C. *Dir.:* Sergio Corbucci. *With:* Terence Hill, Ernest Borgnine, Joanne Dru, Marc Lawrence. **94 mins.** Rated PG. Beta, VHS **($59.95).** Embassy. ★½
   Policeman Hill is exposed to radioactive emissions from a rocket explosion and develops all of the superpowers you've ever read about, including the capacity for flight, which he uses against notorious criminal kingpin Marc Lawrence.

SUPERGIRL (1984) C. *Dir.:* Jeannot Szwarc. *With:* Helen Slater, Faye Dunaway, Peter O'Toole, Ted Wass. **114 mins.** Rated PG. Beta Hi-Fi, VHS Hi-Fi **($79.95).** USA. ★★
   This halfhearted attempt to initiate a new superseries introduces the "last survivor of Krypton's" comely cousin on a mission to save a populated fragment of her planet lodged near our earth's core! The babbling scenario of this turkey (released to theaters, appropriately, at Thanksgiving) involves Supergirl's attempt to retrieve her city's priceless mood stone—the Omegahedron—from a third-rate carnival witch Selena (Dunaway), who's using it to make her dreams of world conquest come true. Slater is appealing in her film debut, and Dunaway offers a serving of ham so juicy you can't help admiring her audacity.

SUPERMAN: THE MOVIE (1978) C. *Dir.:* Richard Donner. *With:* Christopher Reeve, Margot Kidder, Marlon Brando. **144 mins.** Rated PG. Beta, VHS **($69.95);** Laser **($34.98);** CED **($29.98).** Warner. ★★★½
   This big-budget, epic-scale filming of the Superman legend, from the destruction of Krypton to Clark Kent's arrival at the Daily Planet, is overblown but irresistibly entertaining. Mario Puzo's script is oddly schizophrenic, with the elegiac and fabulous first third leading into a breezy confrontation with comedic criminals Gene Hackman and Ned Beatty. Reeve (in his film debut) and Kidder are perfectly cast in this highly satisfying confection.

SUPERMAN II (1980) C. *Dir.:* Richard Lester. *With:* Christopher Reeve, Margot Kidder, Terence Stamp. **127 mins.** Rated PG. Beta, VHS **($69.95);** Laser **($34.98);** CED **($29.98).** Warner. ★★★½

The first sequel picks up where its predecessor began, with Stamp and fellow supercriminals escaping the Phantom Zone and plotting their revenge on the son of Jor-El. Lester imbues the proceedings with subversive humor, but this doesn't detract anything from what is a superb translation of comic-book literature to film, with a memorable no-holds-barred battle in the streets and skies of Metropolis. Romantic subplot features Superman forsaking his powers—at the worst possible moment—for the privilege of bedding Lois Lane.

Superman

Swamp Thing

SUPERMAN III (1983) C. *Dir.:* Richard Lester. *With:* Christopher Reeve, Richard Pryor, Annette O'Toole, Robert Vaughn. **125 mins.** Rated PG. Beta Hi-Fi, VHS **($69.95);** Laser **($39.98);** CED **($39.98).** Warner. ★★½

Electronics genius Pryor, caught embezzling by a crooked employer, is blackmailed into building a supercomputer capable of perverting Superman's values with doses of kryptonite. This movie's bad reputation is only half-deserved; the "bad Superman" footage is embarrassing and never quite bad enough, with his evil registered less by deeds than by browning hair and a greening costume. After some hilarious, slapstick opening credits, Pryor's antics come as a disappointment, but O'Toole's romance with Clark Kent is remarkable for its awkward tenderness and ambiguity.

SWAMP THING (1982) C. *Dir.:* Wes Craven. *With:* Adrienne Barbeau, Louis Jourdan, David Hess. **91 mins.** Rated PG. Beta, VHS **($69.95)**; Laser **($34.95)**; CED **($29.98)**. Embassy. ★★

The story of DC Comics' existential anti-hero—a scientist transformed into a walking bog after ingesting experimental chemicals and becoming immersed in an ecologically contaminated lake—doesn't gel at all on the big screen. It gets off to a fine start, with Craven displaying good command, but falls apart well before the potion turns suave Jourdan into a papier-mâché hedgehog in a fur boa! Barbeau's tough-as-nails act isn't well suited for heroic prominence, either.

SWARM, THE (1978) C. *Dir.:* Irwin Allen. *With:* Michael Caine, Katherine Ross, Richard Widmark. **116 mins.** Rated PG. Beta, VHS **($59.95)**. Warner. ★

The longest and stupidest of the big-budget bee movies, starring half a dozen of Hollywood's best semi-retired actors (Henry Fonda, Fred MacMurray, Olivia de Havilland, etc.) in the roles they'd most like to forget. This preposterous disaster epic has a gigantic swarm of South American bees descending—as they *shall* someday, we are warned—on America, putting the sting to the script's riotous excuse for everyday life. The salaries on this film must've been incredible.

SWORD AND THE SORCERER, THE (1982) C. *Dir.:* Albert Pyun. *With:* Lee Horsley, Kathleen Beller, Simon MacCorkindale. **100 mins.** Rated R. Beta, VHS **($39.95)**; Laser **($34.98)**. MCA. ★★½

This sword-and-sorcery saga follows Prince Horsley's fall from regality and the ensuing sword-slinging revolt against the heinous demon Xusia. The film attracts and rewards interest on an unassuming scale, and never becomes overinflated with self-importance like many of its kind. Special makeup effects by Rick Baker protégé Greg Cannom, some evil-looking set designs, and an overall freshness make this one of the better minor fantasies of recent years.

TALES OF TOMORROW I (1953) B/W. *Dir.:* Various. *With:* Leslie Nielsen, Lon Chaney, Jr., Bruce Cabot. **120 mins.** No rating. Beta, VHS **($49.95)**. Nostalgia Merchant. ★★½

Kinescopes of the first teleseries to treat SF-fantasy seriously. Contains "Frankenstein," "Dune Roller," "Appointment on Mars," and "Crystal Egg." An interesting group, with Chaney's bizarre-looking Frankenstein monster of especial historical interest.

TALES OF TOMORROW II (1953) B/W. *Dir.:* Various. *With:* Boris Karloff, Paul Newman, Rod Steiger, Walter Abel. **120 mins.** No rating. Beta, VHS **($29.95).** Nostalgia Merchant. ★★½

The second of three volumes of the original SF teleseries, this one featuring "Past Tense," "A Child Is Crying," "Ice From Space," and "The Window." A unique opportunity to witness the great Karloff in live performance.

TENTH VICTIM, THE (1965) C. *Dir.:* Elio Petri. *With:* Ursula Andress, Marcello Mastroianni, Elsa Martinelli. **92 mins.** No rating. Beta, VHS **($59.95).** Embassy. ★★★

In the 21st century, violence is legalized in the form of "The Big Hunt," a televised, lethal cat-and-mouse game that rewards the delivery of a hunter's tenth victim with a million dollars. Andress and Mastroianni are, respectively, American and Italian participants whose contest is a spirited metaphor for the battle of the sexes (not to mention political ideologies). A camped-up, SF satire that has aged well and looks ahead to films like *Death Race 2000*.

TERMINATOR, THE (1984) C. *Dir.:* James Cameron. *With:* Arnold Schwarzenegger, Linda Hamilton, Michael Biehn, Paul Winfield. **108 mins.** Rated R. Beta, VHS **($79.95).** Thorn EMI. ★★★½

The murderous cyborg Schwarzenegger is sent backwards in time from a technology-dominated future to 1984, where he must assassinate the mother of the leader of a future human resistance movement. Relentlessly tracked by her heartless assailant through an almost nonstop chain of breathless action scenes, Hamilton is helped by a friend of her unborn son, who makes sure that she lives to conceive in more ways than one. One of the best SF features of recent years, a true feature-length comic book that loses its freshness only during a too-predictable detour through a time-warp romance.

TESTAMENT (1983) C. *Dir.:* Lynne Littman. *With:* Jane Alexander, William Devane, Roxana Zal. **89 mins.** Rated PG. Beta, VHS **($59.95);** Laser **($29.95);** CED **($29.95).** Paramount. ▢® ★★★½

The best of many recent American films about survival in a

nuclear wasteland is a modest portrayal of suburban families pulling together for strength, moving away to less dangerous shores, watching themselves disintegrate, and burying their own. The film doesn't shirk its moral responsibility in favor of spectacular Hollywood mushroom cloud imagery, choosing instead to admire (without glorifying) human love and resilience. The cast is excellent, particularly Alexander describing to daughter Zal the experience of sexual intercourse that she will never live to have, in a story that quite correctly doesn't answer unanswerable questions.

The Terminator   Testament

THEM! (1954) B/W. *Dir.:* Gordon Douglas. *With:* James Whitmore, Edmund Gwenn, Joan Weldon, James Arness. **94 mins.** No rating. Beta, VHS **($59.95).** Warner. ★★★★

The discovery of a catatonic child wandering alone through New Mexico's White Sands desert leads police and scientists to a nest of giant mutant ants, born as a result of 1945 atomic tests performed in the area. Despite the tacky-sounding premise, this is one of the *great* SF films, with a noble humanitarian sentiment and superb, involving performances. The story unravels like an irresistible mystery, laced with terrific visual and verbal puns which help the film play even better the second time around.

THEY SAVED HITLER'S BRAIN (1963) B/W. *Dir.:* David Bradley. *With:* Audrey Caire, Walter Stocker, Carlos Rivas. **81 mins.** No rating. Beta, VHS **($54.95).** VCI. ★½

Originally titled *Madmen of Mandoras,* this landmark of barrel-bottom filmmaking is actually composed of two movies— an unfinished espionage fantasy (circa 1963) about Nazis taking orders from Hitler's severed head to expose the world to nerve gas, and even cheaper, home-movie inserts (circa 1967) that keep things rolling like the proverbial square tire. This mindboggling curio is hilariously hard to follow, with the story leaping from hemisphere to hemisphere, from the past to the distant past, and from bare competence to incompetence. VCI's miserable transfer of film to tape makes the experience even *more* impenetrable!

THIEF OF BAGDAD, THE (1924) B/W. *Dir.:* Raoul Walsh. *With:* Douglas Fairbanks, Julanne Johnston, Anna May Wong. **143 mins.** Silent. No rating. Beta, VHS **($49.98)**. Blackhawk. ★★★

The first, silent version of this Arabian Nights tale follows the dashing Fairbanks on his quest to prove his worth to a Caliph's beautiful daughter. It's an awfully long time for a modern viewer to go without sound, but the special effects and set design by William Cameron Menzies are still highly effective, and include monsters, a winged horse, and the famous flying carpet sequence. The script was co-written by Fairbanks himself under the pseudonym "Elton Thomas."

THIEF OF BAGHDAD, THE (1978) C. *Dir.:* Clive Donner. *With:* Peter Ustinov, Roddy McDowall, Terence Stamp. **100 mins.** Rated G. Beta, VHS **($59.95)**. Video Gems. ★½

This excruciatingly dull, badly cast, made-for-TV version of the story offers absolutely nothing in the way of variety, but special effects followers may wish to check out the contribution made by *Star Wars'* John Stears. If you must see it, do so in ignorance of its two predecessors; it might lend this rusty production an illusion of polish.

THING, THE (1982) C. *Dir.:* John Carpenter. *With:* Kurt Russell, Wilford Brimley, Donald Moffat. **108 mins.** Rated R. Beta, VHS **($79.95)**; Laser **($29.98)**; CED **($29.98)**. MCA. ★★★★

This half-remake of *The Thing from Another World* wisely returns to the original source material (John Campbell's story "Who Goes There?") and gives us something more mind boggling than "an intellectual carrot." An alien creature, capable of assuming the form of any living thing, appears at an arctic military base, resulting in roller coaster scares and grand scale paranoia. Maligned during its brief theatrical run for Rob Bottin's avalanche of slimy special effects, this is nevertheless Carpenter's richest film to date, with more thrills than you'd normally find in ten movies.

THING (FROM ANOTHER WORLD), THE (1951) B/W. *Dir.:* Christian Nyby. *With:* Kenneth Tobey, Margaret Sheridan, James Arness. **80 mins.** No rating. Beta, VHS **($34.95)**; CED **($19.98)**. Nostalgia Merchant. ★★★★

A group of airmen and scientists stationed at an arctic base discover and unearth a frozen alien carcass from the ice, which thaws when a nervous watchman covers the icky sight with an electric blanket. The creature then goes on a rampage for blood. Arness is reportedly ashamed of his participation in this production, easily one of the 15 to 20 best SF films ever made, but his presence is always effective and never less than alarming. We may never know if the film's producer Howard Hawks contributed to its direction, but it's chock full of his own signatures (the camaraderie in the face of ambush, the ostentatious gal, the cute nicknames) and Nyby never made another movie half as good.

THINGS TO COME (1936) B/W. *Dir.:* William Cameron Menzies. *With:* Raymond Massey, Ralph Richardson, Cedrick Hardwicke. **92 mins.** No rating. Beta, VHS **($19.95).** Media. ★★★½

This elaborate filming of H.G. Wells' *The Shape of Things to Come* is the most ambitious and epic SF film of its decade, so long ago that Wells himself was a visitor to the set! The story takes the viewer decade by decade through a remarkably accurate dramatization of the World War to come. The storyline ends in 2036, when the ruling war mongers have been unseated by a more sensible, progress-oriented scientific community determined to send man into space. Magnificently designed (also Menzies' contribution), weakened only by a prevailing air of overtheatricality and preachiness.

THIS ISLAND EARTH (1955) C. *Dir.:* Joseph Newman. *With:* Jeff Morrow, Rex Reason, Faith Domergue. **86 mins.** No rating. Beta, VHS **($39.95).** MCA. ★★★

Renowned scientist Cal Meacham (Reason) receives a mysterious catalogue in the mail offering, free of charge, the materials necessary to build a communications device as yet uninvented by man. This is just the beginning of a terrific, colorful interplanetary adventure that leads Reason and his lost love Domergue from the service of aliens to the distant, war-ravaged planet Metaluna. The special effects are excellent and the drama is tense. Many of the best scenes were directed, sans credit, by SF great Jack Arnold. Must be seen on a color set.

THX-1138 (1971) C. *Dir.:* George Lucas. *With:* Robert Duvall, Donald Pleasence, Johnny Weissmuller, Jr. **88 mins.** Rated PG. Beta, VHS **($39.98).** Warner. ★★★

Lucas' first feature is an expansion of his student film *THX-1138 4EB* (1967), depicting at a tedious length a dehumanized, underground future civilization where sex has been chemically deemphasized. Duvall (in one of his first major film roles) goes off his medication, experiences sex with Maggie McOmie, then eludes the underworld's robot patrolmen in a race to the earth's surface. The other side of the *Star Wars* coin, brimming with originality but without sufficient warmth of character to help its ideas get across to the viewer.

TIME AFTER TIME (1979) C. *Dir.:* Nicholas Meyer. *With:* Malcolm McDowell, Mary Steenburgen, David Warner. **112 mins.** Rated PG. Beta, VHS **($39.98).** Warner. ★★★

H.G. Wells invents a time machine, which is used by one of his friends (Jack the Ripper, on the lam from authorities) to flee into the future. When the machine reappears in Wells' home empty, the author pursues the criminal into the unremorsefully violent 1970s. The atmosphere and performances here are so charismatic (particularly Steenburgen's star-making role) that only afterwards does one recall that Wells was actually an infamous womanizer, and hardly the staid, antiquarian twit portrayed in the film.

Time After Time

Time Bandits

TIME BANDITS (1981) C. *Dir.:* Terry Gilliam. *With:* John Cleese, Sean Connery, David Warner. **110 mins.** Rated PG. Beta Hi-Fi, VHS **($39.95);** Laser **($29.95);** CED **($19.98).** Paramount. ★★½

A parentally ignored boy has his life changed one night when a horse charges through his bedroom closet, signaling an open window in time. This wonderful start portends a true successor to *The Wizard of Oz,* but quickly descends into a series of unfunny historical dalliances, with the boy and a band of time-traveling dwarves meeting Napoleon and Robin Hood, riding the Titanic, and becoming pawns in a contest between Evil (Warner) and the Supreme Being (Ralph Richardson). Some nicely imagined effects only intensify the disappointment of this needlessly sour story.

TIME MACHINE, THE (1960) C. *Dir.:* George Pal. *With:* Rod Taylor, Yvette Mimieux, Alan Young, Whit Bissell. **103 mins.** No rating. Beta, VHS **($59.95);** Laser **($34.95);** CED **($29.98).** MGM/UA. ★★★★

The classic H. G. Wells story is brought warmly to life in this George Pal production. Taylor, weary of the prevalence of war on the last day of the 19th century, celebrates New Year's Eve in his newly invented time machine, in which he witnesses WWII, nuclear war in 1966 (a quaint, forgivable error), and the far-future enslavement of the human race by subterranean cannibals. A richly speculative SF classic, that rare film that stimulates thought as it entertains, then gently pokes you for not believing such a combination was possible.

TIME MACHINE, THE (1978) C. *Dir.:* Henning Schellerup. *With:* John Beck, Priscilla Barnes, Andrew Duggan, Whit Bissell. **99 mins.** Rated G. Beta, VHS **($54.95).** VCI. ★½

A numbing, *Classics Illustrated* version of Wells' classic which, as we all remember, was full of computers and nuclear weapons and turtleneck sweaters. Computer genius Beck's time machine project is temporarily scuttled in favor of developing war weapons, leading him to escape into a distant future akin to that shown in Pal's original, but filmed on a shoestring in Utah. Whit Bissell plays the same character in both versions!

TIMERIDER (1983) C. *Dir.:* William Dear. *With:* Fred Ward, Belinda Bauer, Peter Coyote. **94 mins.** Rated PG. Beta, VHS **($59.95);** CED **($34.98).** Pacific Arts. ★★

A stunt cyclist accidentally steers into the path of a time-travel experiment being conducted in the California dunes, finding himself transported to the Old West. Produced and scored (with anonymous hard rock) by Michael Nesmith, following the success of his video album *Elephant Parts,* the film is disappointingly unadventurous and uncreative. Solid casting is the only commendable element.

TIN MAN (1982) C. *With:* Timothy Bottoms, Deana Jurgens, Troy Donahue. **95 mins.** Rated PG. Beta, VHS **($59.95).** Media. ★★½

Deaf computer genius Bottoms develops "Osgood," a unique computer that can hear and speak for him. Fantasy premise is present long enough to involve the viewer, then subsides into a pleasantly warm romantic drama with introduction of speech therapist Jurgens. Fine work from Bottoms carries the picture.

TOBOR THE GREAT (1954) B/W. *Dir.:* Lee Sholem. *With:* Charles Drake, Karin Booth, Billy Chapin. **77 mins.** No rating. Beta, VHS **($39.95).** Republic. ★½

The inventor of Tobor, the world's first emotional robot, is abducted along with his grandson by a spy ring desirous of his scientific know-how. Guess who saves the day? Sholem directed many of the George Reeves *Superman* episodes, which have universal appeal, but his work here is best suited for those who don't recognize "Tobor" as a reverse spelling.

TOM CORBETT, SPACE CADET VOLUME I (1950-56) B/W. *Dir.:* Various. *With:* Frankie Thomas, Al Markim, Jan Merlin, Frank Sutton. **90 mins.** No rating. Beta, VHS **($19.95).** Nostalgia Merchant. ★½

A compendium of six 15-minute episodes from the earliest days of televised science fiction. Set in the not-too-distant future, the series followed the characters Tom Corbett, Roger Manning, and Astro (not a dog, by the way) through daily disciplines at the Space Academy, where they are being educated to become members of the Solar Guards. As with *Space Patrol* and other tapes hailing from this era, these live kinescopes are best viewed as nostalgia or historic curiosities.

TOM CORBETT, SPACE CADET VOLUME II (1950-56) B/W. *Dir.:* Various. *With:* Frankie Thomas, Al Markim, Jan Merlin, Frank Sutton. **120 mins.** No rating. Beta, VHS **($19.95).** Nostalgia Merchant. ★½

Same as *Tom Corbett, Space Cadet Volume I,* except contains four 30-minute episodes.

TRANSATLANTIC TUNNEL, THE (1935) B/W. *Dir.:* Maurice Elvey.
With: Richard Dix, Leslie Banks, Madge Evans. **70 mins.** No
rating. Beta, VHS **($44.95).** Budget. ★★

An unusual thirties SF about the gruelling construction of an
undersea tunnel connecting America and Great Britain plays disappointingly. The good idea (and possibly reputation) are due to
the existence of the little-seen German classic *Der Tunnel,* made
only one year earlier. The remake boasts an interesting look, but
forfeits its visionary angle to mundane romantic conflicts.

TRIAL, THE (1963) B/W. *Dir.:* Orson Welles. *With:* Anthony
Perkins, Jeanne Moreau, Akim Tamiroff. **118 mins.** No rating.
Beta, VHS **($44.95).** Budget. ★★★½

Perkins is K., a young man arrested in his apartment and taken
into custody without being told the nature of his alleged crime.
Welles' adaptation of Kafka's existential classic is an unceasing
nightmare of man's self-loss in the crush of near-future technology and bureaucracy. Full of perplexing characters and asides
which conjure the book's mercurial atmosphere to perfection, the
film never forfeits Welles' own unmistakable identity as one of the
cinema's great stylists.

TRON (1982) C. *Dir.:* Steven Lisberger. *With:* Jeff Bridges, Bruce
Boxleitner, David Warner. **96 mins.** Rated PG. Beta, VHS
($84.95); Laser **($34.95);** CED **($19.98).** Disney. ★★★

Bridges is a computer genius who illegally enters a computer
system to prove himself the rightful inventor of several stolen
game patents. The super-computer then *absorbs* him into a
bizarre netherworld of video-game warfare. This complex but
lighthearted film has overwhelming computerized special effects
(deserving of an Oscar but not nominated!) and startling, multi-
leveled religious resonance. A brave picture deserving of public
reappraisal.

20,000 LEAGUES UNDER THE SEA (1954) C. *Dir.:* Richard
Fleischer. *With:* Kirk Douglas, James Mason, Peter Lorre. **127
mins.** Rated G. Beta, VHS **($39.95);** CED **($19.98).** Disney.
★★★★

This classic Disney film of the Jules Verne tale has a 19th
century scientist and his associates investigating rumors of a
ship-wrecking sea monster but finding instead a fabulous
submarine commandeered by embittered Capt. Nemo (Mason).

This attractive, richly produced feature is best viewed on the big screen, but is captivating on video nonetheless, thanks to Fleischer's serious grasp of the material and hearty performances. Nemo's pet seal is one of the best co-stars Douglas has ever had.

TWILIGHT ZONE: THE MOVIE (1983) C. *Dir.:* John Landis, Steven Spielberg, Joe Dante, and George Miller. *With:* Vic Morrow, Scatman Crothers, John Lithgow. **101 mins.** Rated PG. Beta, VHS **($69.95);** Laser **($34.98);** CED **($34.98).** Warner. ★★½
   This feature film version of Serling's teleseries, helmed by four of fantasy filmdom's best young directors, is wildly unbalanced but ultimately worthwhile. Landis' episode, about racist Morrow's punishment at the hands of his own prejudice, is severely weakened by its accident-related incompletion. Spielberg's "Kick the Can" is a mild and sentimental fantasy of oldsters rediscovering their youth, literally, in childhood games. The film is stolen outright by Dante's incredible "It's a Good Life," an expressionistic masterpiece about a paranormal, cartoon-loving kid who's turned his home into a three-dimensional Chuck Jones catastrophe. After this, you might not be able to concentrate on Miller's "Nightmare at 20,000 Feet," but it's second-best—a flamboyant and wildly kinetic play on man's fear of flying.

2001: A SPACE ODYSSEY (1968) C. *Dir.:* Stanley Kubrick. *With:* Keir Dullea, Gary Lockwood, William Sylvester. **141 mins.** Rated G. Beta, VHS Hi-Fi **($69.95);** Laser **($39.95);** CED **($39.95).** MGM/UA. ★★★★
   Kubrick's magnificent, legendary, eliptic film begins with a prehistoric tableaux depicting the discoveries of tools, weapons, and murder of one's own kind—then jumps ahead into space, *then* jumps ahead into…? The three panels of this triptych share the common element of a mysterious black monolith, evidence of an otherness in the galaxy. As everyone holding this book must know, it's the high watermark of the science fiction film genre and is likely to remain so for some time.

2010: THE YEAR WE MAKE CONTACT (1984) C. *Dir.:* Peter Hyams. *With:* Roy Scheider, John Lithgow, Helen Mirren, Keir Dullea. **116 mins.** Rated PG. Beta Hi-Fi, VHS **($79.95).** MGM/UA. ★★★

2001: A Space Odyssey

2010: The Year We Make Contact

This attractive sequel to Kubrick's *2001: A Space Odyssey* has the intimidating responsibility of improving upon Genesis, but meets the challenge honorably. A Russian-American space expedition is sent into orbit around Jupiter to investigate some mysterious problems on the *Discovery,* unmanned since pilot Bowman's disappearance into the planet's atmosphere. The special effects are stunning, but this is certainly no actor's showcase, with low marks going to a bland Scheider as the American mission leader, and a severe Mirren as his Soviet counterpart.

TWO WORLDS OF JENNIE LOGAN, THE (1979) C. *Dir.:* Frank DeFelitta. *With:* Lindsay Wagner, Marc Singer, Linda Gray. **100 mins.** No rating. Beta, VHS **($49.95).** USA. ★★

A woman discovers an antique dress in her newly purchased house which fits so perfectly that it sends her back in time, where she falls in love with an artist whom she knows will die in a duel in 1899. A made-for-TV fantasy for Harlequin romance fans— another obsessive indulgence in the reincarnation theme by one-track director DeFelitta, author of *Audrey Rose* and *The Entity.* Wagner is as good as always—too good for material like this.

UNDERSEA KINGDOM (1936) B/W. *Dir.:* B. Reeves Eason and Joseph Kane. *With:* Ray "Crash" Corrigan, Lois Wilde, Lon Chaney, Jr. **260 mins.** No rating. Beta, VHS **($N/A).** Nostalgia Merchant. ★★

Entertainingly silly Republic serial about the struggles between Sharad (William Farnum) and the diabolical Khan (Monte Blue) in the sunken kingdom of Atlantis. Corrigan, playing himself in the kind of adventure he presumably had off screen all the time, joins forces with Sharad and finds romance and combat amid assorted sets and costumes with Neptunian motifs. Best remembered today for early supporting performance by Lon Chaney, Jr., in a costume that's half-gladiator, half-Flash Gordon.

UP THE SANDBOX (1972) C. *Dir.:* Irvin Kershner. *With:* Barbra Streisand, David Selby, Jane Hoffman. **97 mins.** Rated R. Beta, VHS **($39.98)**. Warner. ★★★

As a neglected housewife bracing herself for the news of a third pregnancy, Streisand subjects herself to a feature-length immersion in fantasies expressive of her insecurities. At a cocktail party, her breasts swell towards men, and her pregnant stomach swells as she meets her husband's mistress. Streisand's only box-office failure is, ironically, one of her best outings, boasting a good script, an inspired performance, and no singing.

VARAN THE UNBELIEVABLE (1962) B/W. *Dir.:* Inoshiro Honda. *With:* Myron Healey, Tsuruko Kobayashi, Kozu Nomura. **70 mins.** No rating. Beta, VHS **($34.95)**. VCI. ★½

Another prehistoric terror emerges from the lakes of Tokyo, courtesy of Healey's backfired experiment with chemically tainted water. Actually filmed in 1958, with several American scenes added in 1962, this tape has an opening sequence which credits only the American crew! Healey is surprisingly good, but the rest of the film is pretty ordinary.

VIDEODROME (1983) C. *Dir.:* David Cronenberg. *With:* James Woods, Deborah Harry, Sonja Smits. **87 mins.** Rated R. Beta, VHS **($59.95)**; Laser **($29.98)**. MCA. ★★★★

Cable TV executive Woods monitors pirated telecasts of a "snuff" program, featuring masochists tortured to death on camera, and learns too late that the signal causes brain tumors, and that these tumors induce bizarre hallucinations. A multidimensional masterpiece that works brilliantly as SF, horror, and satire, with the cast becoming gradually engulfed in a grisly wonderland of Rick Baker makeup effects. Videotape and discs restore the controversial footage deleted from the theatrical version.

VILLAGE OF THE DAMNED (1960) B/W. *Dir.:* Wolf Rilla. *With:* George Sanders, Barbara Shelley, Michael Gwynne. **78 mins.** No rating. Beta, VHS **($59.95)**; CED **($29.98)**. MGM/UA. ★★★

A compelling, well-acted film of John Wyndham's novel *The Midwich Cuckoos* begins with everything within the confines of the illage falling asleep, later awakening to an illusion of normalcy that disappears when 12 women are found pregnant with rapidly maturing fetuses. The identically blonde children are birthed on the same day, and their talents shortly reveal them to be an insidious form of alien invasion. Martin Stephens, as David (the central child), played another diabolical boy in *The Innocents*.

VILLAGE OF THE GIANTS (1965) C. *Dir.:* Bert I. Gordon. *With:* Tommy Kirk, Johnny Crawford, Ronny Howard, Beau Bridges. **80 mins.** No rating. Beta, VHS **($59.95)**. Embassy. ★★

Little Ronny is a genius whose preteen shenanigans with his chemistry set produce a red mousse called "goo" which enlarges anything that ingests it to gigantic size. When two humongous, slam-dancing ducks disrupt The Beau Brummels' set at the neighborhood disco, thrill-seeking delinquent teens cop the goo and put the town under their thumb. Hilarious, mildly sexy SF-fantasy from Mr. B.I.G. is based on H.G. Wells' *The Food of the Gods* (but you knew that from the synopsis, right?), and makes for wonderful low entertainment.

VIRUS (1980) C. *Dir.:* Kinji Fukasaku. *With:* Glenn Ford, George Kennedy, Chuck Connors. **106 mins.** Rated PG. Beta, VHS **($59.95)**. Media. ★½

The actors listed above are just a fraction of an all-star cast assembled for this immense SF-disaster film, the most costly production in Japanese history (which, of course, was entrusted to the director of *The Green Slime*!). A stolen germ-warfare virus is fumbled by its hijackers, exposed to the air, and kills all life on the Earth, apart from 864 men and 8 women stationed in the Antarctic. Whatever seriousness the story might have had is obscured by an endless parade of famous faces, making the apocalypse a sort of bizarre, pop-art collage.

VISIT TO A SMALL PLANET (1960) B/W. *Dir.:* Norman Taurog. *With:* Jerry Lewis, Joan Blackman, Earl Holliman. **85 mins.** No rating. Beta, **($29.95)**. Musicvision. ★★½

Lewis is sensitive, boneheaded alien Kreton (get it?), who plays hooky from his home planet to indulge his fascination with all things earthly. Gore Vidal's original satire took an outsider's point of view to make a commentary on the foibles of the human race, but this movie is more of a commentary on the art of slapstick. Decent entertainment, with some classic Jerry Lewis bits, such as his wild reactions to the entertainment offered at a beatnik nightspot.

VISITOR, THE (1979) C. *Dir.:* Michael J. Paradise (Giulio Paradisi). *With:* Glenn Ford, Mel Ferrer, Shelley Winters, Joanne Nail. **90 mins.** Rated R. Beta, VHS **($69.95);** CED **($29.95).** Embassy. ★½
A muddled Italian-American picture that melds elements from *Close Encounters* and *The Omen,* with extraterrestrial John Huston exercising his influence over a young mother and her Antichrist child. It has an intermittently attractive look, suffused with a plush, blue atmosphere, and quite a roster of guest stars (Sam Peckinpah, Glenn Ford, Mel Ferrer), all of whom appear just long enough to die in the middle of a special-effects spectacle. Nail, recognizable from American TV commercials, keeps her end of the production *relatively* stable—in this instance, quite an accomplishment.

VOYAGE TO THE BOTTOM OF THE SEA (1961) C. *Dir.:* Irwin Allen. *With:* Walter Pidgeon, Barbara Eden, Peter Lorre, Frankie Avalon. **105 mins.** No rating. Beta, VHS **($59.98).** CBS/Fox. ★★½
Pidgeon plays Admiral Nelson, designer of the fabulous atomic submarine Seaview, who is drafted to use his ship to douse the flaming Van Allen radiation belt surrounding the earth. The interesting cast is caught up in a variety of distracting intrigues, a faulty formula that was given full reign in the subsequent teleseries, but the movie is a much tauter ship and probably Allen's most restrained piece of filmmaking.

WAR GAME, THE (1967) B/W. *Dir.:* Peter Watkins. *With:* Michael Aspel, Dick Graham. **47 mins.** Beta, VHS **($34.95).** Hollywood Home Theater. ★★★★
A harrowing, pseudodocumentary short about the political, hygienic, and social results of a nuclear explosion in Great Britain. Originally filmed for the BBC, which refused to broadcast it because it was too intense for public consumption. A superb piece of work, piercingly brief and to-the-point.

WAR OF THE WORLDS (1953) C. *Dir.:* Byron Haskin. *With:* Gene Barry, Ann Robinson, Carolyn Jones. **85 mins.** No rating. Beta,

VHS **($59.95)**; Laser **($29.95)**; CED **($19.98)**. Paramount.
★★★½

George Pal produced this brilliant and colorful adaptation of Wells' Martian invasion story, which features some of the most intimidating alien spacecrafts and technology you'll see anywhere (in fact, the aliens themselves are barely glimpsed, wearing their ships as heartless extensions of themselves). The special effects, building brilliantly from the Martians' hatching from a meteor to a pleasingly ironic defeat, are given proper prominence over a requisite love story between Barry and Robinson. Grade-A production has sense of wonder that Pal delivered better than anyone.

WARLORDS OF THE 21ST CENTURY (1982) C. *Dir.:* Harley Cokliss. *With:* Michael Beck, Annie McEnroe, James Wainwright. **91 mins.** Rated R. Beta, VHS **($69.95)**; Laser **($29.95)**; CED **($29.95)**. Embassy. ★★½

A mysterious loner (Beck) comes to the rescue of a vegetarian commune when it is threatened by the ingenious villain Stryker (Wainright), designer of a deadly "battletruck". This New Zealand-made *Road Warrior* clone barely clears low expectations on the strength of several fine performances and somber, thoughtful direction.

WARRIORS OF THE WASTELAND (1983) C. *Dir.:* Enzo G. Castellari. *With:* Timothy Brent, Fred Williamson, Anna Kanakis. **92 mins.** Rated PG. Beta, VHS **($69.95)**. Thorn EMI. ★

A terrible combination of *My Bodyguard, The Road Warrior,* and *The Warriors* has two musclebound protectors guarding innocent bystanders against 21st century hoodlums. As with Castellari's semi-sequel *1990: The Bronx Warriors,* a laughable exercise in macho excesses, full of tough-guy dialogue and exploding weapons.

WATCHER IN THE WOODS, THE (1980) C. *Dir.:* John Hough. *With:* Bette Davis, David McCallum, Lynn-Holly Johnson, Carroll Baker. **84 mins.** Rated PG. Beta, VHS **($69.95)**. Disney. ★★½

A composer's family moves into a mysterious cottage owned by a gnomic woman (Davis). The eldest daughter notices the onset of psychic communications directed at her from the house's mirrors and the adjoining woods. Hough *(The Legend of Hell House)* knows how to use atmosphere, and sustains it quite well here, despite Johnson's inability to seem special enough for psychic receptivity.

WAVELENGTH (1983) C. *Dir.:* Mike Gray. *With:* Robert Carradine, Cherie Currie, Keenan Wynn. **87 mins.** Rated PG. Beta, VHS **($69.95);** Laser **($34.95).** Embassy. ★★½

Woodsman Carradine encounters drifter Currie, whose hypersensitivity allows her to "overhear" silent cries for help from aliens imprisoned by the U.S. Government for experimental purposes. This low-budget drama is a pleasant surprise, written and directed by *China Syndrome* author Gray, with both acting leads contributing interesting and offbeat characterizations. The aliens are actually bald black children painted blue, and the tinny, electronic score is by Tangerine Dream.

Westworld

The Wizard of Oz

WESTWORLD (1973) C. *Dir.:* Michael Crichton. *With:* Richard Benjamin, Yul Brynner, James Brolin. **88 mins.** Rated PG. Beta, VHS **($59.95);** CED **($29.98).** MGM/UA. ★★★

An adult amusement park offers its customers three robotized milieux in which to live out their fantasies—Medievalworld, Romanworld, and Westworld—the latter of which is chosen for a weekend by suburban buddies Brolin and Benjamin. They drink with robots, sleep with robots, shoot it out with robots, and then must fight for their lily-livered lives when the park loses control over homicidal "Yul Brynner in *The Magnificent Seven*" robot. This clever situation develops into a riveting SF-suspense piece, sharpened by the inspired casting of Brynner, good effects, and an incisive message about the dark side of male fantasies.

WHEN WORLDS COLLIDE (1951) C. *Dir.:* Rudolph Maté. *With:* Barbara Rush, Richard Derr, Peter Hanson. **81 mins.** No rating. Beta, VHS **($49.95)**; Laser **($29.95)**. Paramount. ★★★

An arresting end-of-the-world scenario; adapted from an Edwin Balmer-Philip Wylie novel, finds Earth caught in a collision course with another planet with mankind's only hope of survival being a Noah's Ark expedition to an approaching planet's oxygen-rich moon. The cast is competent but never as interesting as their situation; it's all very civilized, with the Ark crew being chosen by lottery. A George Pal production with generally good effects.

WHERE TIME BEGAN (1978) C. *Dir.:* J. Piquer Simon. *With:* Kenneth More, Pep Munne, Jack Taylor. **87 mins.** Rated G. Beta, VHS **($69.95)**. Embassy. ★

This Spanish remake of *Journey to the Center of the Earth* is a dreary descent all around, with More looking worn and out of place amid the expected parade of photographically enlarged lizards and man-in-suit monsters. The scenery and special effects—the strongholds of the 1959 version—are shamefully cheap and uninspired, but it *does* go the original one better by dispensing with the Pat Boone musical numbers.

WIZARD OF MARS, THE (1964) C. *Dir.:* David L. Hewitt. *With:* John Carradine, Roger Gentry, Vic McGee. **81 mins.** No rating. Beta, VHS **($39.95)**. Republic. ★

It's high school drama night in space, as four astronauts scale and paddle through the red rocks of Mars toward an ancient city. It's there that Carradine—the film's only professional actor—all too briefly appears as a wizard determined to keep them stranded on his own turf. It's hard to imagine why this excruciatingly dull SF rewrite of *The Wizard of Oz* needed a technical adviser, but Forrest J. Ackerman did something to earn that questionable honor.

WIZARD OF OZ, THE (1939) C. *Dir.:* Victor Fleming. *With:* Judy Garland, Ray Bolger, Bert Lahr. **101 mins.** Rated G. Beta, VHS Hi-Fi **($59.95)**; Laser **($34.95)**; CED **($29.95)**. MGM/UA. ★★★★

One of Hollywood's quintessential productions, this Technicolor musical adaptation of L. Frank Baum's classic is so well known that it's transcended the need for description. Without a doubt the most beloved fantasy film of all time, it was a television favorite before the video revolution, and is even better without commercial interruptions. Stereo has recently been added to the videocassette editions, making this title a must for anyone interested in screening fantasy's best at its best.

WOMAN IN THE MOON, THE (1929) B/W. *Dir.:* Fritz Lang. *With:* Gerda Maurus, Willy Fritsch, Fritz Rasp. **112 mins.** Silent. No rating. Beta, VHS **($55.00).** Festival. ★★★

Lang's follow-up to the magnificent *Metropolis* was this prophetic drama about the first lunar expedition, which made the first speculations (astonishingly correct) about rocket-powered interplanetary travel. The film's rocket plans (courtesy of Willy Ley) were so accurate, in fact, that Hitler had all available prints burned because of their proximity to secret German weapons of the thirties! This silent film loses its momentum, however, after arrival on the moon, which is depicted as a hilly pickpocket's wonderland, with gold nuggets and diamonds glittering everywhere.

X: THE MAN WITH THE X-RAY EYES (1963) C. *Dir.:* Roger Corman. *With:* Ray Milland, Diana Van Der Vlis, Dick Miller. **80 mins.** No rating. Beta, VHS **($59.95).** Warner. ★★★

Milland is Dr. Xavier who uses experimental eyedrops on himself to enhance the range of his vision. Instead, he develops the ability to see through solid objects—a talent that changes his status from scientist to faith healer to sideshow freak to social outcast. One of Corman's best and most intelligent productions, with an unforgettably potent final curtain. Don Rickles is quite good in a supporting dramatic performance.

YOR: THE HUNTER FROM THE FUTURE (1983) C. *Dir.:* Anthony M. Dawson (Antonio Margheriti). *With:* Reb Brown, Corinne Clery, Alan Collins. **88 mins.** Rated PG. Beta, VHS **($79.95);** Laser **($29.95);** CED **($29.98).** RCA/Columbia. ★

A prehistoric hunk rescues a curvaceous cavewoman from a dinosaur menu, then both of them are hurled into the distant future by a mysterious amulet around his neck. Everything about this tedious, noisy Italian production—from the postnuclear deserts presided over by the evil Overlord to the phony special effects—indicate an absolute nullity of imagination and creativity. Director Margheriti began his career in the early sixties with stylish horror films, but he quickly fell into a pattern of shooting any script that fell into his hands.

ZAPPED (1982) C. *Dir.:* Robert J. Rosenthal. *With:* Scott Baio, Willie Aames, Heather Thomas. **98 mins.** Rated R. Beta, VHS **($39.95);** Laser **($34.95);** CED **($19.95).** Embassy. ★½

This theatrical vehicle for popular TV heartthrob Baio is juvenile (but, you'll notice, *R-rated*) piffle about a chemistry whiz who, through a miscalculation, causes an explosion and develops telekinetic abilities. At the school prom and elsewhere, a lot of chesty schoolgirls get their brassieres popped, causing Baio to blush and Aames to snicker. Baio may have made *Stoned,* an anti-pot TV movie, but he indulges quite contentedly here.

Yor: The Hunter From the Future   Zapped

ZARDOZ (1974) C. *Dir.:* John Boorman. *With:* Sean Connery, Charlotte Rampling, Sara Kestelman. **105 mins.** Rated R. Beta, VHS **($59.98).** Key. ★★★

Connery is wonderful as Zed the Exterminator, one of a race of macho primitives who worship the weapons spewed at them daily by a gigantic, floating stone head. Zed's religious curiosity leads him to stow away inside its mouth, and he soon arrives in the Vortex, an intellectual but sexless place where he becomes a stud and the spearhead of a genetic revolution. This ambitious SF satire is magnificently photographed by Geoffrey Unsworth *(2001),* but crumbles somewhat after an unexpected and unsatisfying explanation of events.

ZELIG (1983) B/W & C. *Dir.:* Woody Allen. *With:* Woody Allen, Mia Farrow, Stephanie Farrow. **79 mins.** Rated PG. Beta, VHS **($79.95);** Laser **($34.98);** CED **($19.98).** Warner. ★★★½

A mockumentary about the life and times of 1930s celebrity Leonard Zelig, whose neuroses enabled him to physically become whatever type of person he associated with. A brilliant feat of cinematic legerdemain, incorporating Allen and Farrow into old photos, newsreel footage, and historical incidents. Running commentary by such luminaries as Saul Bellow, Bruno Bettelheim, and Susan Sontag builds to a predictable parallel with the faceless followers of Fascism, but the point is well made and the movie is a classic example of experimental entertainment.

ZOMBIES OF THE STRATOSPHERE (1952) B/W. *Dir.:* Fred C. Brannon. *With:* Judd Holdren, Aline Towne, Leonard Nimoy. **260 mins.** No rating. Beta, VHS **($N/A).** Nostalgia Merchant. ★½

This 12-part Republic serial is the second and final Commando Cody adventure, with Holdren harnessed in the "Up-Down-Fast-Slow" jetpack and fisting it out with invading aliens. The exceptionally tired, shoddy production seems half-filled with stock footage from vintage cliffhangers. This entry has accidentally landed in the cult books due to the auspicious casting of young Nimoy as a repenting alien invader. A shorter, more bearable feature version is available under the title *Satan's Satellites*.

DIRECTORY OF VIDEO SUPPLIERS

Admit One Video
311 Adelaide St. East
Toronto, Ontario
Canada M5A IN2

Blackhawk Films
1235 West Fifth
Box 3990
Davenport, IA 52808

Budget Video
1534 North Highland
#108
Hollywood, CA 90028

Catalina Home Video
7962 10th Street
Suite 101
Westminster, CA 92683

CBS/Fox Video
1211 Avenue of the Americas
New York, NY 10036

Cultvideo
8160 Amor Road
Los Angeles, CA 90046

Embassy Home Entertainment
1901 Avenue of the Stars
Los Angeles, CA 90067

Family Home Entertainment
Internat'l. Video Entertainment
7920 Alabama Avenue
Canoga Park, CA 91304

Festival Films
2841 Irving Ave. South
Minneapolis, MN 55408

Hollywood Home Theater
4590 Santa Monica Blvd.
Los Angeles, CA 90029

Key Video
1298 Prospect Ave.
La Jolla, CA 92037

King of Video
3529 S. Valley View
Las Vegas, NV 89103

K-tel Video
11311 K-tel Dr.
Minnetonka, MN 55343

Maljack Productions, Inc.
15825 Rob Roy Dr.
Oak Forest, IL 60452

MCA Home Video
70 Universal City Plaza
Universal City, CA 91608

Media Home Entertainment
5730 Buckingham
Culver City, CA 90230

MGM/UA Home Video
1350 Avenue of the Americas
New York, NY 10019

Monterey Home Video
International Video Entertainment
7920 Alabama Ave.
Canoga Park, CA 91304

Nostalgia Merchant
5730 Buckingham
Culver City, CA 90230

Pacific Arts Video Records
PO Box 22770
Carmel, CA 93922

Paragon Video Productions
3529 South Valley View
Las Vegas, NV 89103

Paramount Home Video
5555 Melrose Ave.
Los Angeles, CA 90038

Prism
1875 Century Park East
Suite 1010
Los Angeles, CA 90067

RCA/Columbia Home Video
2901 W. Alameda
Burbank, CA 91505

Republic Pictures Home Video
12636 Beatrice St.
Los Angeles, CA 90066

Sony Corporation
Video Software Operations
9 West 57th St.
New York, NY 10019

Thorn EMI
(now **Thorn EMI/HBO**)
1370 Avenue of the Americas
New York, NY 10019

Touchstone Home Video
500 South Buena Vista St.
Burbank, CA 91521

USA Home Video
International Video Entertainment
7920 Alabama Ave.
Canoga Park, CA 91304

VCI Home Video
(now **United**)
6535 East Skelly Dr.
Tulsa, OK 74145

VCL Home Video
3660 San Vicente Blvd.
Suite 301
Los Angeles, CA 90048

Vestron Video
1011 High Ridge Rd.
PO Box 4000
Stamford, CT 06907

VidAmerica Inc.
235 East 55th St.
New York, NY 10022

Video City Productions
4266 Broadway
Oakland, CA 94611

Video Dimensions
110 East 23rd St.
Suite 603
New York, NY 10010

Video Gems
731 North La Brea Ave.
PO Box 38188
Los Angeles, CA 90038

Video Yesteryear
Box C
Sandy Hook, CT 06482

Warner Home Video Inc.
4000 Warner Blvd.
Burbank, CA 91522

Walt Disney Home Video
500 South Buena Vista St.
Burbank, CA 91521

Wizard Video Inc.
948 North Fairfax Ave.
Los Angeles, CA 90046

Worldvision Home Video Inc.
660 Madison Ave.
New York, NY 10021